Critical Guides to French Texts

11.40

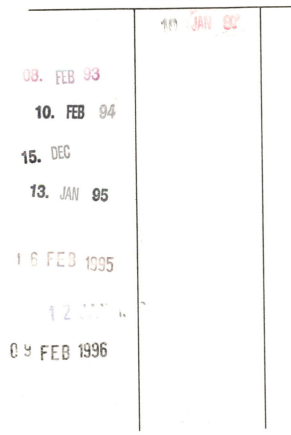

Critical Guides to French Texts

EDITED BY ROGER LITTLE, WOLFGANG VAN EMDEN,
DAVID WILLIAMS

ZOLA

L'Assommoir

Valerie Minogue

Research Professor in French
University College of Swansea

Grant & Cutler Ltd
1991

© Grant & Cutler Ltd
  1991
ISBN 0-7293-0333-0

I.S.B.N. 84-401-2066-4

DEPÓSITO LEGAL: V. 1.551 - 1991

Printed in Spain by
Artes Gráficas Soler, S. A., Valencia

for

GRANT & CUTLER LTD
55-57, GREAT MARLBOROUGH STREET, LONDON W1V 2AY

28/10/93(0)

Contents

Prefatory Note

T H E method I have adopted in this short study has arisen from my own responses to the text and to the vision of reality (reality of vision?) I there perceive. This personal reading does not pretend to be comprehensive, nor does it attempt a survey of the vast quantity of existing critical work. I should, however, like to acknowledge here my great debt and gratitude to previous critics whose ideas I have both consciously and unconsciously absorbed, and whose perceptions and scholarship have been invaluable in the preparation of this study. I should also like to express my gratitude to University College, Swansea, for the sabbatical leave which made this work possible, and to Professor Roger Little for his very helpful comments and advice.

References to *L'Assommoir* in brackets in the text are to the Folio edition* of *L'Assommoir,* edited and annotated by

* For those using other paperback editions I give below a table of concordance which should help with the tracing of page-references. In the table, F refers to the Folio edition above, GF to the Garnier-Flammarion edition (*L'Assommoir,* chronologie et introduction par Jacques Dubois, Paris, Garnier-Flammarion, 1969), and LP to the Livre de Poche (*L'Assommoir,* préface de François Cavanna, commentaires et notes de Auguste Dezalay, Paris, Livre de Poche, 1983). Roman numerals refer to chapters.

F: I, p. 19; II, p. 52; III, p. 86; IV, p. 123; V, p. 158; VI, p. 198; VII, p. 236
GF: I, p. 35; II, p. 62; III, p. 90; IV, p. 120; V, p. 149; VI, p. 182; VII, p. 213
LP: I, p. 9; II, p. 41; III, p. 75; IV, p. 111; V, p. 145; VI, p. 183; VII, p. 221

F: VIII, p. 281; IX, p. 325; X, p. 371; XI, p. 414; XII, p. 461; XIII, p. 499
GF: VIII, p. 250; IX, p. 286; X, p. 324; XI, p. 360; XII, p. 399; XIII, p. 430
LP: VIII, p. 265; IX, p. 309; X, p. 353; XI, p. 395; XII, p. 441; XIII, p. 477

Henri Mitterand, with a preface by Jean-Louis Bory, Paris: Gallimard, 1978. Other works are indicated by the italicized numbers they bear in the Bibliography.

V. M.

Introduction: Scientific Observation and Poetic Vision

L'ASSOMMOIR, published in 1877, is the seventh of the twenty novels that make up Zola's Rougon-Macquart cycle (1871-93). The very vastness of the enterprise says much about the robust vitality of Zola's creative energy, and the popularity of his novels shows Zola's capacity for seizing the attention and imagination of a wide public. His popularity has, however, to some degree, worked against his artistic reputation. He has been accused of lacking style, of being crude, repetitious and over-emphatic, a pseudo-scientist with a taste for sensationalism and morbid sexuality. It is true that Zola builds massively rather than working in delicate filigree and traces of morbid sexuality are not hard to find in his novels. Violence abounds, and there are repetitions, but the repetitions are used very effectively to underline similarities or contrasts, and they play a vital role in the orchestration of his work. In the last few decades, the image of Zola as a crude, popular craftsman has given way to a deeper appreciation of his art and the rich patterns of his mythopoeic imagination. [1]

Zola had not always been the apparently harsh realist of *L'Assommoir.* He had earlier seen himself primarily as a poet and his youthful verse and stories reveal a taste for the lyrical and the fantastic, whether fairy-tale or nightmare. These early writings bear the impress of his childhood in the Provençal countryside and his enthusiastic readings of the Romantic poets. In his mature works, there is a fruitful tension between his poetic impulse and his effort to achieve veracity and

---

[1] Some of the most influential critical work on this aspect of Zola may be found in *15, 18, 19, 28, 30, 33, 35, 36, 37,* and in anthologies such as *11, 13, 21, 31.*

apparent objectivity, and between the epic sweep of his imagination and his concern for exactitude in the prosaic details of
everyday life.

Zola's realism, or 'naturalism', as he preferred to call it,
was a logical continuation from the realism of Balzac and
Flaubert, who had already turned the literary focus on to
aspects of life – money, mediocrity, the lower social ranks –
which earlier writers had generally shunned. Zola's 'naturalism' involved inclusion of the sterner realities of life, and the
presentation of 'ordinary' characters from all levels of society.
Instead of being exceptional and cultivated individuals whose
complex inner life takes precedence over all else, Zola's characters are drawn from the ordinary run of humankind, and
securely rooted in specific times, places and activities. 'Le
premier homme qui passe', said Zola, 'est un héros suffisant;
fouillez en lui et vous trouverez certainement un drame simple
et qui met en jeu tous les rouages des sentiments et des passions' (see *28*, p. 34). This statement of 1866 is qualified, in
the 'Notes générales sur la nature de l'œuvre' (1868-69), by
Zola's clear acknowledgement of the validity and even necessity of exceptional elements – 'L'œuvre gagne en intérêt humain
ce qu'elle perd en réalité courante. Il faudrait donc faire excep-
tionnel comme Stendhal, éviter les trop grandes monstruosi-
tés, mais prendre des cas particuliers de cerveau et de chair'
(*2*, V, p. 1743).

Even with allowance made for the exceptional, the demo-
cratic option for the ordinary poses considerable literary problems. If the main characters of a novel are non-intellectual,
inarticulate and rather lacking in sensitivity, their responses to
their experience may prove rather uninteresting. For a novelist
like Zola, whose cultivation of impersonality forbids obvious
authorial intervention in the novel, this is a particularly
thorny problem. The novelist has to compensate for the inade-
quacies of his characters without himself taking the centre of
the stage to comment and reflect on events. Zola evolved a
number of effective strategies, as we shall see, to provide this
'compensation'.

The 'naturalist' novelist was to present a recognizable reality, paying careful attention to economic, political, social and

physical factors, and viewing human life in the light of recent scientific discoveries. Science in Zola's day offered a great many new insights and ideas, not all of which were accurate, but most of which were stimulating and challenging to one like Zola in passionate pursuit of the truth of his times. Science and documentation, however, never ousted imagination and poetry for Zola; he would view the world with a scientist's gaze, but through the eyes of a poet. The fact that he so often used the term 'poème' to refer to his novels in his preliminary notes indicates the persistence of Zola's poetic intention. There is a sense in which Zola may be said to poeticize Science itself. It becomes one of the great forces that Man must harness and use in what Zola sees as the great human struggle to achieve full dignity and restore the lost majesty of mankind.

Zola's readings of Darwin on evolution, his study of Letourneau's *Physiologie des passions,* which linked the emotional and physical sides of Man, and his study of Prosper Lucas's *Traité philosophique et physiologique de l'hérédité naturelle* gave him a number of important and stimulating guidelines. His imagination would of course assert its own rights, but would respect available scientific truths, acknowledge Man's physical constitution, and show a strong sense of the interdependence of body and spirit. Zola's attachment to the scientific exploration of this interdependence may be judged by his agreeing to submit himself to an extraordinarily rigorous physiological and psychological examination conducted by a team of experts and lasting over a year – the very detailed and often fascinating results were published by Edouard Toulouse *(38)* in 1896. The 'scientific' view of Man as an evolving animal, subject to the motions of his blood, the resistance or weakness of his flesh, the shaping force of his environment, and the dispositions inherited from his ancestry, curbed and balanced Zola's exuberant and lyrical view. If Man, in Zola's vision, was a great spiritual force, almost a god in the universe, he was also, in the determinist view Zola adopted from the influential philosopher-critic, Hippolyte Taine, a product of 'race, milieu et moment' – heredity, environment and moment in time.

Zola's formulation of his aesthetic, while it advocates an unblinking respect for truth, fully acknowledges that 'observation' is not a totally unproblematic process. When Zola opts to view the world through the 'realist screen', he insists, in a letter of 1864, that whatever its pretensions, no 'screen' can be merely transparent. Even the realist screen has its own distorting (but creative) peculiarities: 'des propriétés parti-culières qui déforment les images, *et qui, par conséquent, font de ces images, des œuvres d'art...*' (my italics; see *14*, pp. 21-22). In the polemical work, *Le Roman expérimental,* which appeared in 1880, three years after *L'Assommoir,* Zola assumes a more intransigently 'scientific' stance. Applying the arguments of Claude Bernard's *Introduction à la médecine expérimentale* to the novel, Zola presents the novelist as an observer and experimenter. The 'observer' provides the facts that create the solid platform on which characters and actions will be developed (see *4,* p. 63), and the 'experimenter' sets the plot in motion in accordance with natural laws and ob-served phenomena. But the writer must produce and shape all the events, and here, for Zola, lies the domain of invention and genius.

There is nothing crudely mechanical or photographic in Zola's approach. His faith in science and his belief that the experimental novel can ultimately lead to the understanding and mastery of the determining forces at work in human life, reflect the optimism of the age, but Zola does not naïvely confuse the writer's study with the laboratory: 'nous sommes loin ici des certitudes de la chimie et même de la physiologie' (*4,* p. 64). Slavish observation and *reportage* were, in any case, not Zola's intention; he repeatedly insists on the necessity of a personal vision: 'Un grand romancier est ... celui qui a le sens du réel *et qui exprime avec originalité la nature, en la faisant vivante de sa vie propre'* (*4,* p. 223, my italics. See also p. 218). For Zola, observation and interpretation go hand in hand; even in his preparatory jottings (see his *Carnets* for *L'Assommoir* in *5,* pp. 415-37), observed details rapidly be-come sign and symbol, as Henri Mitterand has admirably demonstrated: 'chaque détail perd son caractère fortuit, et de-vient un signe au sein d'un ensemble' (*33,* p. 72).

The Rougon-Macquart cycle, with its twenty volumes, offers a wide view of French life in Zola's time, depicting diverse episodes in the lives of various members of the Rougon-Macquart family, and relating them to the situation and events of the age. The era on which Zola chose to focus his gaze runs from the *coup d'état* of 1851, when Louis-Napoléon, the nephew of Napoléon I, seized power, until the collapse of his régime and the end of the Second Empire, in 1870. Zola planned to do for the Second Empire what Balzac had done for an earlier period of French history in the novels of the *Comédie humaine.* In taking a family as his focus, Zola was able to develop his themes and ideas not only across the various strata of society, but also from generation to generation. He could show the importance of hereditary elements, the influence of varying environments, and the impact of the historical moment – the Second Empire – which he characterizes in the preface to the first novel of the series as 'une étrange époque de folie et de honte' (*2,* I, p. 4).

Zola's scientific ambitions meant that he would include in his work elements that more delicately selective writers would have omitted. It meant too that he would use – as he does in *L'Assommoir* to great effect – the crude but vigorous language of the working-class, and show all the squalor, violence and depravity of the seedier side of working-class Parisian life, while maintaining the apparently detached attitude of the scientific observer. When it first appeared in serial form – first in *Le Bien public,* then in *La République des Lettres,* from April 1876 to January 1877 – and in book form in 1877, *L'Assommoir* aroused a good deal of outrage and opprobrium. The violence of the novel and the vulgarity of much of its language led to charges of immorality (see, for instance, the attacks of Brunetière and others, collected in *11*). Zola, predictably enough, defended himself in the name of realism and truth, but Zola's view of the truth was too brutal for many of his readers.

In his preface, Zola draws attention to the critical storm his novel provoked, and asserts the morality of his intentions. He clearly felt that the moral thrust of his work was self-evident – he describes it in the *Ebauche* as 'un effroyable

tableau qui portera sa morale en soi' (p. 543) – but his refusal
to make explicit moral judgements within the novel led to
condemnations of his stark depiction of working-class life and
the charge that it was likely to reinforce class-prejudices.[2] The
duty of the novelist, apart from the obvious one of producing
good novels, was, in Zola's view, to present reality and truth
vividly, but it was up to the readers, the legislators and society
at large to draw their own conclusions. Clear moral or political
directives were to be avoided: the text could carry a moral
charge no less powerful for being implicit and integral.

If *L'Assommoir* presents so desperate a picture it is because
Zola has so terrible a truth to present and so vivid a compassion, but to see *L'Assommoir* as merely an expression of nihi-
listic despair, as some have done, is to ignore the insistent
throb of the life-force that accompanies the unequal struggles
of the poor, and the humour and verve of so many scenes. It
is by the force of the imaginative pressure he exerts on an
observed and studied reality that Zola carries that reality into
the moral dimensions of what Peter Brooks has called 'a myth-
ological realm where the imagination can find a habitat for its
play with large moral entities' (*16,* p. 4). What finally im-
presses is the solidity of the world of *L'Assommoir* – its buildings, its language, its trades, its people with their passions and
preoccupations – while a great cry of 'Oh! what a fall was
there!' seems to echo from these pages that tell of human
dignity betrayed and brought low.

No artistic constraints forbade direct speaking in Zola's
journalism, where he depicted the wretchedness of the poor
districts of Paris, and the susceptibility to alcohol encouraged
by the constricting conditions. Addressing the ruling-classes
on the subject of the working-class drunkard, he makes his
moral viewpoint quite explicit: 's'il glisse, s'il roule vers
l'ivrognerie, c'est votre faute... Il prend la joie qu'il a sous la
main, il en abuse, parce que vous lui fermez l'horizon et qu'il
a besoin d'un rêve, fût-ce le rêve de l'ivresse'.[3] That sense of

---

[2] André Kédros's 'Lettre à M. Zola à propos de *L'Assommoir'* (in *25*) is a
vigorous example of denunciation of Zola's 'detachment'.

[3] Article in *Le Corsaire,* 17 Dec., 1872 (cited in *28*, p. 123).

the 'closed horizon'[4] becomes an important part of the thematics of *L'Assommoir* and one of the many strategies by which Zola's supposedly neutral and dispassionate narrative embodies a passionate and compassionate view of the world.

The social-document side of *L'Assommoir* has sometimes obscured its artistic worth, making it the focus of studies mainly concerned with the sociological, historical and political import of the novel. But the enduring strength of Zola's novel lies in its literary quality, by which I mean the patterns it weaves, the density and intensity of the emotions it evokes in its rhythms and images, the sensuous impact it makes on the reader's mind, the myriad things that work directly upon the reader's senses and imagination – even though it may take many readings to track them down and see just how they work.

The solid massiveness of Zola's *œuvre* and the vivid power of his imagination, in fact those qualities that have helped to make him so popular, have, as I suggested earlier, often weighed against him in the literary scales. He has been accused of lacking not only refinement and sensitivity, but style and art and even intelligence. His adherence to theories now outmoded has been held against him, and his characterization has been described (even by some admirers) as rather gross and unperceptive. There are, indeed, no complex analyses of human psychology in Zola's pages, but his characters grip the reader's attention and compel assent with a force that derives from the intensity with which they have been visualized, inwardly grasped and translated into words on the page. Zola's writing (as I shall try to demonstrate in this study), with its sometimes thundering emphases and its vigorous embracing of the crude, the melodramatic, the poetic and symbolic, is directed by a prodigious artist.

With the weight and detail of the physical and everyday world, Zola combines a powerful epic thrust. Solidly based on observation, *L'Assommoir* is above all a masterpiece of ima-

---

[4] The image also occurs in a previous article (cited in the *Dossier, 1*, p. 539), and in *Germinal*, accompanying the idealistic dreams of Gervaise's son, Etienne Lantier: 'C'était, brusquement, l'horizon fermé qui éclatait, une trouée de lumière s'ouvrait dans la vie sombre de ces pauvres gens' (*2*, III, p. 1278).

ginative design and construction. The poetic richness of Zola's sensuous, emotional and moral response to the world about him gives an organic vitality to his picture of Parisian life, and endows the characters and events with a significance beyond themselves, a mythic quality that links the particular to the universal and gives to the everyday incident a place in a human drama of epic scale.

1

The Web of Circumstance

T H E events and characters of Zola's novels are set at the centre of many interweaving strands which together give intensity and density to the narrative. The shaping forces of the environment, the role of heredity, and the importance of the historical moment – which might so easily create a heavy and inert background – become active and dramatic elements in the texture of the fictional lives.

L'Assommoir takes hold of the reader from the very first page, on which we meet Gervaise in tears, waiting for the return of Lantier. From that opening scene of misery and apprehension, things move quickly to their quarrel and Lantier's abandonment of her. She is left with their two children in an alien environment which we see through her eyes in her early-morning vigil. Paris seems from the outset a vast impersonal ocean carrying tides of people into its cavernous mouth, depositing some, like flotsam, at street-corners and bars.

The scene of Gervaise's struggle for survival is set, and the reader is immediately involved in the desperate plight of the 'heroine' – not because she is delicate, beautiful and helpless, but because she is a vulnerable human being in a hostile and even monstrous situation. Her situation is fairly banal – a young unmarried mother abandoned by her lover. Zola, however, makes us experience it as monstrous, making a 'creative exploitation' (*34,* p. 4) of some of the devices of melodrama and popular fiction – sharp contrasts, heightened and forceful language – to create a supercharged atmosphere, in which all the elements of the scene participate in the drama, and objects acquire symbolic status.

Such intensifying devices operate in the opening pages to make an immediate impact on the reader. The contents of

Gervaise's room, from the chipped water-jug to the 'flancs vides' of the trunk in the corner, and the little heap of pastel pink pawn-tickets on the mantelpiece all speak of wretched poverty. Outside, rotting shutters and crumbling plaster tell the same story. The wind carries from the abattoir 'une odeur fauve de bêtes massacrées', while on the other side stands the hospital on whose roofs Coupeau will work, and where later he will be a patient before going on to die at Sainte-Anne. At night, in this district of dark alleys and filth, Gervaise hears 'des cris d'assassinés': death seems to threaten on all sides. As dawn breaks, Gervaise's isolation is heightened as she watches a great tide of men, beasts and carts rolling down to the city. The march of the human 'herd' mingles suggestively with the odour of slaughtered animals and Zola here runs two metaphors together, the 'herd' and the larger 'flood' which bears it along: 'Il y avait là un piétinement de *troupeau,* une foule que de brusques arrêts *étalaient en mares* sur la chaussée... et la cohue s'engouffrait dans Paris où elle *se noyait,* continuellement' (p. 21, my italics). Whereas in sensationalist fiction, objects, images and violent impressions are wheeled on like stage-props for immediate effect and then forgotten, the images and impressions that Zola creates in this first scene are threads that will be woven into the fabric of the whole novel.

There will be, in Zola's fictional world, no supremely evil villains directing events, though the dehumanized brutality of Bijard serves to show to what depths of mindless depravity a human being may sink. There will be no simple but satisfying triumph of the good, nor even (with the exception of Lalie Bijard) the pitiful spectacle of innocent goodness destroyed by wickedness. There is no 'happy ending', nor is Gervaise's fate merely the result of villainous machinations. Gervaise is 'une figure sympathique' but 'chacune de ses qualités tourne contre elle. Le travail l'abrutit, sa tendresse la conduit à des faiblesses extraordinaires', as Zola writes in the *Ebauche* (*2,* II, p. 1545). For all her unimportance in the general scheme of things – a laundress of less than impeccable morals – she becomes, in Zola's treatment, an epic and tragic figure, bearing a fatal flaw and opposed by overpowering impersonal forces. The forces of her destiny are not part of a supernatural order such as that

which makes Racine's Phèdre succumb to 'Vénus tout entière
à sa proie attachée'. But just as Phèdre is 'fille de Minos et de
Pasiphaé', so Gervaise is 'fille de Macquart et de Joséphine'.
Her heredity, the milieu in which she struggles to survive, and
the historical moment in which she lives will be the forces of
her destiny. The naturalist should, ideally, show us with equal
detachment and precision the anatomy of the fly and the proce-
dures of the spider that traps it. While Zola observes acutely,
and remains apparently detached, he uses all his art to evoke
and express compassion for the human fly caught in the web of
circumstance. The 'scientific' elements of the world of *L'Assommoir* are seen 'à travers un tempérament', and where we
might have been offered scientific disquisitions on heredity,
and a dry analysis of the contemporary social and political
background, Zola gives us the living, physical and concrete
details of the everyday experience of an individual, thus giving
organic life to the three strands – heredity, environment and
historical moment – of the determinist web.

i)   HEREDITY

Heredity is not presented as a theory, in conceptual terms,
but as a particular family history, made palpable and visible
in Gervaise's lame leg. That family history begins in Plassans
(Aix-en-Provence, where Zola was born) with Gervaise's
grandmother, Adélaïde Fouque, born in 1768. Adélaïde's
father had died insane, and she was herself subject to nervous
disorders and attacks of hysteria which increased in violence
as she grew older. Through 'tante Dide', as she is known, Zola
adds an element of inbuilt drama to the life of all her progeny.
A question mark hangs over them all – will they succumb to
the hereditary flaw? Tante Dide marries one of her workmen,
Rougon, and bears him a son. When Rougon dies, she takes
Macquart as her lover and bears him first a daughter, then a
son, Antoine, who marries Joséphine Gavaudan and becomes
the father of Gervaise of *L'Assommoir*, Lisa of *Le Ventre de
Paris*, and Jean of *La Terre* and *La Débâcle*. As Antoine is a
drunkard, this illegitimate side of the family inherits a double

threat – mental disorder and alcoholism. If Zola's concern was in part that of a 'scientific' observer, the structure he adopted for the Rougon-Macquart cycle of novels reflects far more than a merely documentary or scientific interest. As Angus Wilson remarks: 'The vision of a wandering brood, sprung from a tainted stem, burrowing and fighting its way through the shaking structure of the glittering Empire has a violent and dramatic quality' (*40*, p. 103).

The shadow of heredity looms particularly large and dark over Gervaise, since not only did both her parents drink, but the limp with which she is afflicted from birth is presented, in the first novel of the cycle, as a direct result of the drunken brawling nights of her parents: 'Conçue dans l'ivresse, sans doute pendant une de ces nuits honteuses où les époux *s'assommaient,* elle avait la cuisse droite déviée et amaigrie, étrange reproduction héréditaire des brutalités que sa mère avait eu à endurer dans une heure de lutte et de soûlerie furieuse' (*2*, I, p. 124, my italics). The verb 'assommer', which presides in the title of Gervaise's novel, makes an early appearance in her life, and alcohol is, for Gervaise, as Jacques Dubois succinctly puts it, 'son signe du zodiaque, il scelle son destin' (*23*, p. 21). Her mother Joséphine, known as 'Fine' (itself a familiar French term for brandy), introduces Gervaise to the anisette to which she is herself addicted, and in her early teens Gervaise often ends up, along with her mother, sunk in a drunken stupor (*2*, I, p. 142). Other maternal traits also reproduce themselves in Gervaise, and the relation between her mother and father in many ways prefigures that between Gervaise and Coupeau in its later stages. Zola gives early warning of the resemblance between Gervaise and her mother in Gervaise's conversation with Coupeau (pp. 58-60) during their first visit to the 'Assommoir' when Gervaise also confesses her youthful drinking. Alcohol now revolts her. She is hardworking, eager to fulfil her very modest ambitions and, as Coupeau comments, 'une belle et brave femme'.

Her will and energy carry her some way towards fulfilment of her ideal, and her lameness – that outward and visible sign of the inner flaw – becomes almost imperceptible in her days of bustling vitality. Then, as life and circumstances press in upon her, the 'douceur d'agneau' inherited from her mother, 'qui avait servi de bête de somme au père Macquart pendant plus de vingt ans' (p. 58), and the innate weakness for alcohol, together perform their work of corruption, converting what had been easy-going good nature and tolerance into sloth, while self-indulgence, drink and obesity exaggerate the limp to the point where, in the closing stages of the novel, it becomes a grotesque deformity and Gervaise a hideous caricature of herself.

When the will is sapped, the inherited tendencies take over and run riot, as if depersonalizing the individual. The *blanchisseuse* with her blonde prettiness and capable, pink, dimpled arms becomes an amorphous monstrosity. And Zola makes sure that when we see Gervaise in her degradation we are not allowed to forget the woman she once was: 'Elle était bien gentille, blonde et fraîche, en ce temps-là' (p. 483). With that memory fresh in the mind of both Gervaise and the reader, we see her, at the end of the novel, contemplating her hideous shadow as she walks the streets: 'Elle louchait si fort de la jambe, que, sur le sol, l'ombre faisait la culbute à chaque pas; un vrai guignol!' (p. 488): it is the lame leg with all the symbolic force of its 'étrange reproduction héréditaire' that is in the ascendant here like the evil star of her destiny.

The forces of heredity also bear upon Coupeau, whose father fell from a roof while drunk. Coupeau, nicknamed 'Cadet-Cassis' because of his avoidance of spirits, falls from the roof-top while sober. He then succumbs to drink partly because he develops a taste for the easy life Gervaise creates for him after his accident, and partly because of embittered resentment of his misfortune, coupled with an inherited predisposition. Just as Zola reminds us, in Gervaise's downfall, of her earlier days, Zola introduces a reminder of Coupeau as a young *zingueur* into the horror of the 'danse macabre' in which *delirium tremens* leads him, mindless, to his death. As Gervaise, appalled, watches his wild antics in his cell, they suddenly make a pattern she recognizes: 'Gervaise comprit qu'il s'imaginait être sur un toit, en train de poser des plaques de zinc ... Oui, son métier lui revenait, au moment de crever' (p. 511). The memory of the healthy, good-natured and skilful Coupeau is dramatically superimposed on his hideous death-dance, to show the crippling, disfiguring effects of heredity and alcoholism.

If skills and personal qualities are submerged at last in the triumphant flow of hereditary currents, Zola shows, in the course of the novel, how those hereditary forces may be countered by personal effort with the help of a suitable environment. When Coupeau spends three months out of Paris, 'où il y a dans les rues une vraie fumée d'eau-de-vie et de vin' (p. 373), he stops drinking, and is temporarily restored to health. In his preface to L'Assommoir, Zola tells us he will paint 'la déchéance fatale d'une famille ouvrière, dans le milieu empesté de nos faubourgs'. The environment has a very powerful role, and that use of 'nos' points to a shared responsibility for what happens to humanity in the miseries tolerated by society.

The stunted lives of L'Assommoir will bear their bitter fruits in the lives of Gervaise's children, related in L'Œuvre, Germinal, Nana and La Bête humaine. (Gervaise's son Jacques, the murderer of La Bête humaine, who falls victim to alcohol and madness, was added to the family retrospectively – a singular example of painless childbirth!) It is noticeable that Gervaise's daughter, Anna Coupeau – Nana – is more Lantier than Coupeau. Zola had picked up from Prosper Lucas the (false) notion that a woman's first lover impregnated her once and for all. This made it virtually impossible for her to resist his advances at any stage, and her children would always be his. When relatives cluster round the baby Anna, they see nothing of Coupeau in her: 'la petite n'avait rien de Coupeau ... ces yeux-là ne venaient pas de la famille' (pp. 130-31). Not merely Nana's eyes but her character traits derive from Lantier; she will be a consumer, even devourer, just like her 'father'. Nana will be depicted, in the novel that bears her name, as a Golden Fly bred in the social swamps tolerated by an irresponsible and pleasure-seeking society, a fly that carries the vengeance of pestilence into the upper reaches of society. The childhood and adolescence of Nana, notably in Chapter XI, become a platform for the later novel, in which Nana's bitter memories of her early life serve as weapons in her subjugation and humiliation of her aristocratic lover, Count

Muffat. *L'Assommoir* not only works out, through Gervaise herself, the consequences of a tainted heredity in a hostile environment, but it shows the formation of further tainted individuals whose lives will form the substance of other novels in the cycle.

ii) THE HISTORICAL MOMENT

In the scheme of the Rougon-Macquart series, *L'Assommoir* is the novel of the Paris working-class. Zola had intended to make it the political novel he had long projected, but he changed his mind: 'Le roman de Gervaise n'est pas le roman politique, mais le roman des mœurs du peuple; le côté politique s'y trouvera forcément, mais au second plan et dans une limite restreinte' (*2,* II, p. 1546). It was with *Germinal* that Zola was to raise a more decisively political voice, but the 'côté politique' in *L'Assommoir,* although limited, still provides an implicit but powerful denunciation of the political régime that tolerated and, in Zola's view, even aggravated the conditions he describes.

There is an undertow of political references in the novel that draws attention, above all, to the exclusion of the working-classes from any say in political matters. Political issues of the time (1850-68) are not so much reflected as refracted through the ill-informed gossip of the milieu, and arguments are often voiced by characters for whom the reader will have scant respect. The ignorant and opinionated M. Madinier holds forth; the petty, mean and egoistic Lorilleux expresses political views largely based on the fact that he shares a birthday with the comte de Chambord[5] and therefore associates the possibility of good fortune with the royalist cause...! Some facts do filter through the fog of ignorance and ineptitude, as when anger is expressed at the law of May 31, 1850 (p. 112) by which three years of fixed residence were required to qualify for the

[5] Duc de Bordeaux, grandson of Charles X; head of the legitimist party and claimant to the French throne in 1870-71.

right to vote (though M. Madinier reports it as two years). The effect of this law was to exclude from the vote large numbers of workers who had recently moved into the city. M. Madinier blames the politicians for this and reports that Bonaparte himself is 'très vexé, car il aime le peuple' (p. 112). Though claiming to be a Republican, he (like many others) supports Louis Bonaparte out of respect for his prestige as the nephew of the great Napoleon. In the later part of the novel, however, scandal flows freely around the figure of the Emperor, and the company at Gervaise's *fête* is regaled with titbits from a scurrilous work *Les Amours de Napoléon III,* complete with illustrations, including one of the Emperor, bare-legged but wearing the sash of the Légion d'Honneur, in lascivious pursuit of the daughter of one of his cooks. Poisson, always loyal to the Emperor, is dismayed, but forced to believe it since 'C'était dans un livre, il ne pouvait pas dire non' (p. 292). Such exchanges show up the naïve gullibility of the people and the dubious authenticity of much of the supposed 'information' available to them.

Lantier is the mouthpiece for a good deal of criticism of the Emperor and his régime, but since Lantier is lazy and parasitic, this strikes the reader as merely the expression of his envious resentment of the Emperor as a rival consumer. Lantier's ideas are formed from incessant nibbling at newspapers backed up by his 'library' of books – a chaotic medley of Louis Blanc (with one volume missing), Lamartine, and Eugène Sue. When Etienne goes off to Lille, Lantier sees him off with a homily about his rights as a worker, and advice which, from him, sounds ludicrous: 'Souviens-toi que le producteur n'est pas un esclave, mais que quiconque n'est pas un producteur est un frelon' (p. 295). Such words are hollow in the mouth of a 'frelon' like Lantier. The very language of political and social comment is stripped of meaning – it becomes mere empty slogan-mongering.

A more genuine social criticism is made obliquely when le père Bru, taking the capacity to work as the sole and necessary justification for his existence, reflects on his present uselessness, as if his age were a capital crime: 'le malheur, c'est que je ne sois pas mort. Oui, c'est ma faute. On doit se coucher et crever, quand on ne peut plus travailler' (p. 265). Lorilleux murmurs confused suggestions about the government's need to create pensions for the 'invalides du travail', while Poisson crushingly responds that 'Les Invalides sont pour les soldats... Il ne faut pas demander des choses impossibles' (p. 265). The sources of these views prevent us from taking them as expressions of the authorial viewpoint, but such garbled discussions allow Zola to point to serious problems and the need to find solutions. The very lack of any serious and informed political discussion or even social comment indicates how far these people are from having any effective political voice.

This could of course be misconstrued, and Zola has been criticized, for instance, for putting anti-Imperialist views into the mouth of Lantier and thus depriving them of significance, but almost all the explicitly social and political discussion is shown to be mere mouthing of common clichés or the striking of self-flattering postures. Zola may well – as he has been accused of doing – have exaggerated the political ignorance of the working classes at this time. If he does, it is an exaggeration that expresses his angry sense of their exclusion from political reality and responsibility. It is not when they are 'talking politics' that their comments cut deep, but when they unself-consciously and almost inadvertently reflect on the reality in which they live. Perhaps the truest reflection of Zola's view of their political status is Coupeau's apathetic comment: 'En voilà une blague, la politique! Est-ce que ça existe pour nous?' (pp. 112-13). From a more sober and measured standpoint, Goujet, with his honest commonsense, shows something of the same scepticism, despite his Republican convictions.

On December 2, 1851, the day of the *coup d'état* by which Louis-Napoléon seized power, Coupeau goes out just to see the fun, but is nearly arrested at the barricades. Goujet comes along in time to help him get away, but takes no part in the fighting, feeling that the game is not worth the candle. Even as he walks away, however, he wonders whether this passivity may prove costly: 'le peuple un jour pourrait se repentir de s'être croisé les bras' (p. 137). Very few workers made any protest at the *coup d'état*. Maurice Descotes claims that Zola even understates the case: 'Le monde ouvrier, dans sa grande

masse, ne demeura seulement pas indifférent: abusé par le
prestige de l'Oncle et la réputation de réformateur social du
Neveu, il accorda le préjugé favorable' (*20,* p. 20). Descotes
quotes the following items from Proudhon's diary: '5 décembre: Le peuple a été presque satisfait. 6 décembre: Tandis
que les bourgeois laissaient faire et passer, les ouvriers applau-
dissaient et défaisaient les barricades...' (*20,* p. 21).

Zola presents his Paris workers as living in a sort of hinter-
land beyond politics. For Gervaise, reality is made up of the
succession of work and meals, births and deaths, celebrations
and sufferings, and ultimately the hopeless misery of cold and
hunger in the slum areas surrounded by Haussmann's recon-
structions. The modernization of Paris, the slum-clearance
and the creation of the straight wide avenues for which Paris
is now justly famous, had been projected even under Louis-
Philippe, but the project was realized in the reign of Napoléon
III at amazing speed and enormous cost, in an atmosphere of
wild speculation, in which fortunes were lost and made over-
night, as Zola showed in *La Curée.* The spectacular nature of
the enterprise and the way in which it was carried out caused
it to be seen by many as above all an expression of the Emper-
or's personal vanity and his desire to leave a lasting monu-
ment, whatever the cost. Certainly Haussmann became the
centre of a storm of criticism: he was, as Henri Mitterand puts
it, 'le symbole d'un régime de pouvoir personnel, de faste, de
corruption, et de mépris des misères populaires' (*2,* I, p. 1572).
The haste of the scheme made life even harder for the poor,
for as buildings and streets disappeared, the remaining habita-
tions of the poor became even more filthy and overcrowded –
ghettos of wretchedness in the midst of the new city.

In a newspaper article in 1868, Zola had written: 'Les
ouvriers s'étouffent dans les quartiers étroits et fangeux où ils
sont obligés de s'entasser. Ils habitent les ruelles noires qui
avoisinent la rue Saint-Antoine, les trous pestilentiels de la
vallée Mouffetard. Ce n'est pas pour eux qu'on assainit la ville;
chaque nouveau boulevard qu'on perce les jette en plus grand
nombre dans les vieilles maisons des faubourgs' (*2,* I, p. 1540).
If Zola's article makes the point eloquently, the comments
gain immeasurably when presented from the viewpoint of one

who is actually living in these conditions, 'les uns sur les autres, dans ces grandes gueuses de maisons ouvrières; on y attraperait le choléra de la misère' (p. 495). In Gervaise's long and terrible wanderings through the streets of Paris in Chapter XII, she contemplates the devastation of the demolition, the great new spaces and the crumbling old houses in the midst of the new buildings: 'Sous le luxe montant de Paris, la misère du faubourg crevait et salissait ce chantier d'une ville nouvelle, si hâtivement bâtie' (p. 479).

In another article, in *La Cloche* in February 1870, Zola castigated the indifference of the régime to the conditions of the poor, pointing to the gross inequalities of wealth so blatantly displayed, and showing his contempt for a rule whose order is maintained by force of arms: 'L'envie du peuple est faite de misère. Vous avez trop de musique, trop de fleurs, et de femmes, et le pauvre a trop de pauvreté. Qu'importe, n'est-ce pas! L'armée est là. Le maître a répondu de l'ordre. Les maréchaux balayeraient les faubourgs, s'ils bougeaient' (cited in *20,* p. 17). For all his studied adoption of a neutral impersonal detachment, the passionate views explicity expressed in Zola's journalism implicitly animate the pages of *L'Assommoir.* Direct expression of political opinions is less important in this novel than the misinformation and clichés of the sporadic political discussions; their very ineptitude speaks clearly of the need for education and information. It is the endurance, the effort, the suffering, the humour, the ignorance and even the depravity of the Paris slums that are made politically eloquent. Through them, Zola proclaims the need for reform and greater social justice.

iii) ENVIRONMENT

It is obvious from the first pages of *L'Assommoir* that there is nothing abstractly scientific about the way Zola presents the milieu in which his characters are enmeshed. The opening, with its picture of the start of the working day, already indicates many features characteristic of Zola's presentation of the city. It shows, for instance, the way Zola captures specific places and particular moments of the day, and the way he combines attention to the mass with attention to the individuals within it. It shows too the way Zola animates his cityscapes, giving them moral and emotional coloration, and it demonstrates the sensuous impact of the scenes he paints. When Zola says in his preface 'J'ai voulu peindre la déchéance fatale d'une famille ouvrière', his choice of the verb 'peindre' is singularly appropriate.

The alternation of panoramic views with close-ups of Gervaise in her miserable room in the Hotel Boncœur is characteristic of similar moves throughout the novel, as is the breaking-up of fairly lengthy descriptive blocks by individual conversations – here, first with Coupeau, then with Mme Boche. Zola ensures that descriptive passages remain in close touch with the protagonists, so that we do not feel, as we do in some nineteenth-century novels, that the novelist is putting the characters temporarily aside to give the reader information or to indulge in word-pictures for their own sake. It is striking that in the opening pages, we see outside only when Gervaise looks out of the window, scanning the streets for Lantier. With these shifts of focus from individual to mass, from inside to outside, and from description to conversation, we also see wide variations in the narrative mode: an apparently neutral authorial overview of events gives way to a filtering of events through the consciousness of a character, or to reported or direct speech. As the novel progresses, the authorial overview becomes more and more infiltrated by the experience and language of the protagonists, thus closing still further the gap between the author and the lives he relates, causing the reader to enter more fully into the world of the characters, and creating the impression, as Henri Mitterand puts it, 'que le livre a été entièrement pensé dans le parler du peuple, et comme rédigé par la voix collective du quartier de la Goutte-d'Or' (2, II, p. 1556).

In this urban novel, Zola captures marvellously the movements of the crowd, the activities and the sense-impressions that characterize particular moments of the day, but such moments are set into a broader perspective. The temporary and contingent stand out against a sense of continuity and history: the Lariboisière Hospital, for instance, is pinned into a wider temporal framework with the brief comment 'alors en construction'. Things are seen existing in time, resisting or succumbing to time's ravages, as is evident in the peeling wall-paper and broken-down furniture in Gervaise's room and the general dilapidation outside. Towards the end of the novel we come back with Gervaise for a final glimpse of the place where it all began, to find the Hotel Boncœur now derelict and the abattoirs in process of demolition. Each hour takes its place in the life of the day, and the day in a long series of days in individual lives and in the lives of successive generations: the moment is thus immediate and particular but also exemplary.

In the opening pages, Gervaise gazes at the dawn scene with a vision coloured by her immediate anguish and by memories of the cries and fears that have disturbed her nights, and the particular scene she views is part of a wider picture. The workers flood by in waves until eight o'clock, when the shops open and only a few latecomers pass: soon it is time for morning constitutionals and for mothers to take their babies out. It is all part of '[le] réveil énorme de Paris' (p. 25) in which the watching Gervaise is but a tiny dot in the huge indifferent life of the city.

In the communal wash-house, where Gervaise confides her history to Mme Boche, the private conversation alternates with a wider view of the rows of women shouting, laughing and cursing in the steam-laden air that smells of soap and bleach. The immediate moment is set in a broader pattern of daily routine, with a lull at eleven when the women stop to eat. In the momentary quiet, the regular scraping of the stoker's shovel is heard and the continuous puffing of the boiler fills the room as if it were the very lungs of the wash-house. In this public context, with its seemingly corporate life, in which individual beings seem but cells in a vaster organism, Gervaise confronts Virginie, the sister of the woman Lantier has taken up with, and a furious fight takes place. The fight finally dispels any notion we might have had of Gervaise as a helpless and delicate creature. The dishevelment of the washerwomen, their vulgarity and coarse jokes, the spiteful malice of Virginie, the avid curiosity of Mme Boche and the blind rage of Gervaise all blend together in the violence of the encounter. Gervaise, as a newcomer, 'n'ayant point encore le coup de gosier de Paris' (p. 43) is at a disadvantage against Virginie's easy flow of insults, but it is Gervaise who triumphs and ends up beating Virginie's bare backside. Zola slots this instant back into the wider frame of Gervaise's life: 'elle se mit à battre, comme elle battait autrefois à Plassans, au bord de la Viorne...' (p. 48). In the midst of an alien world with unfamiliar patterns, Gervaise's identity and continuity are thus reaffirmed. Each big public scene – and there are many – seems to create a double impression of this sort, of a corporate life, with its own customs and calendar, and of individuals within it, pursuing their precarious existences.

When Gervaise has left the wash-house, Zola, in an unusual move, returns us to the scene she has left behind: the washerwomen are back at work, 'les faces allumées, égayées par le coup de torchon de Gervaise et de Virginie' (p. 50). The whole incident, central to Gervaise, is peripheral to the mass-life, simply a part of the day's entertainment. Time moves on to 'le chien de l'après-midi, le linge pilé à coups de battoir... les fumées devenaient rousses' (p. 50), and the scene ends with a shift of focus to the machinery that dominates the 'lavoir' – the huge boiler and the 'bras d'acier' of the engine, that seem to mock the puny efforts of human arms. By thus placing the moments and incidents of Gervaise's day in the broader context of the life of Paris or the life of the *lavoir,* Zola initiates the reader into the crushing indifference of the teeming life around her. Such scenes, however, are more than functional. They have a vividness and immediacy comparable with the paintings of the Impressionists, for whom the colours and light-effects of the particular instant were so important, while they also have the emotional impact associated with the later Expressionism.[6] Zola draws on a broad range of sense-impressions to create tactile effects as well as evoking colour,

---

[6] See, for instance, on Zola's impressionism, P. Hamon in *Cahiers Naturalistes,* no. 34 (1967) and in the same journal, Joy Newton in no. 33 (1967); on expressionism, Joy Newton in no. 41 (1971).

sounds, smells and tastes, and he excels at suggesting movement, capturing tiny gestures, picking out the individual in
the crowd, and the detail in the larger mass.

When Gervaise sits for the first time in the 'Assommoir'
with Coupeau, it is midday. Gervaise has put down her basket
of washed clothes, and the snatched moment is part of a
general intermission in the day's activities. The shops are
about to close for lunch; floors are being swept, the last basket
of chips is being pulled out, plates are being rearranged on
counters, and the workers emerge for the midday break, like
children at play-time, jostling and shoving, sliding on the
pavement in a clatter of hob-nailed boots. Some stand and
smoke reflectively, others blink in the sunlight: together they
form 'un flot paresseux coulant des portes ouvertes, s'arrêtant
au milieu des voitures, faisant une traînée de blouses, de bourgerons et de vieux paletots, toute pâlie et déteinte sous la
nappe de lumière blonde qui enfilait la rue. Au loin, des
cloches d'usine sonnaient...' (p. 59). Such vigorously evocative
pictures, with their colours and sounds and smells, their seizing of overall movement and of tiny but telling gestures, not
only capture the reader's imagination but also serve to anchor
Gervaise and Coupeau in the life and movements of the *quartier*.

Towards the end of the novel, Gervaise's wanderings
through the city create a similar sense of a particular time of
day and relate the solitary individual to the anonymous masses
of the city:

> Le crépuscule avait cette sale couleur jaune des crépuscules
> parisiens, une couleur qui donne envie de mourir tout de suite,
> tellement la vie des rues semble laide. L'heure devenait louche,
> les lointains se brouillaient d'une teinte boueuse. Gervaise, déjà
> lasse, tombait justement en plein dans la rentrée des ouvriers.
> A cette heure, les dames en chapeau, les messieurs bien mis
> habitant les maisons neuves, étaient noyés au milieu du peu-
> ple... (p. 480)

Zola makes the *milieu* come to life for the reader through
the eyes and the emotional response of the characters. This
intertwining of description with emotional effect reveals the

interaction between individuals and milieu without any necessity for theoretical exposition.

The main thrust of Zola's presentation of the urban environment in *L'Assommoir* is to show the indifference or hostility of the city as a whole to the individuals within it, and beyond that, to show the physical and moral squalor of 'nos faubourgs empestés'. The pressures of urban life, especially for the vast numbers of provincials who flocked into Paris in these years, begin to be felt in the squalid room where the novel opens – and which is, we are told, the best room in the Hotel Boncœur. The five-storey apartment-block in the rue Goutte-d'Or, with its three hundred or so tenants, is not just a huge, dirty overcrowded building; like every other part of the environment, it becomes, in Zola's treatment, organic and animate. Seen through the eyes of Gervaise at various stages of her life, it is made to embody the hostile forces that crush her hopes and bring them to destruction.

Her first view of it comes when Coupeau goes to visit the Lorilleux and Gervaise waits for him outside. She sees an enormous mud-coloured cube, 'd'une nudité interminable de murs de prison, où des rangées de pierres d'attente semblaient des mâchoires caduques, bâillant dans le vide' (pp. 64-65). Gervaise's immediate impression of the building as 'un organe vivant' or 'une personne géante', prefigures the role the building will play in her life, like an evil giant from a legend. When Gervaise finally moves into the building with its labyrinthine corridors, she feels the satisfaction of accomplishing at last a long-cherished ambition, but also a chilling dread (p. 158). In its vastness, its disturbing concentration of people and activities, the building looms threateningly before her, and later in the novel she will indeed regret ever having entered into its gaping jaws.

Just as the apartment-block acquires a sinister life of its own, so other pressures of life in the city become live, threatening forces rather than merely ugly facts of the environment. The menace of alcohol, already present in Gervaise's blood, in her early life, and in the visible stigma of her lame leg, is omnipresent in the atmosphere of the city. From the very beginning, we are made aware of the workers who stop and give themselves up to sloth in the wineshops, and Zola highlights the evil power of alcohol in the still in Colombe's bar, and its product, the infamous 'vitriol'. From its first appearance, the *alambic* has an almost supernatural presence; it is 'une cuisine du diable devant laquelle venaient rêver les ouvriers soûlards' (p. 53) and it becomes a devilish machine working inexorably, tirelessly, to extend its domination over the whole city: 'L'alambic, sourdement, sans une flamme, sans une gaieté dans les reflets éteints de ses cuivres, continuait, laissait couler sa sueur d'alcool, pareil à une source lente et entêtée, qui à la longue devait envahir la salle, se répandre sur les boulevards extérieurs, inonder le trou immense de Paris' (p. 62). The machine fills Gervaise with horror at the first encounter and its demonic character later becomes even more apparent: 'l'ombre de l'appareil, contre la muraille du fond, dessinait des abominations, des figures avec des queues, des monstres ouvrant leurs mâchoires comme pour avaler le monde' (p. 409).

Without departing from a basic realism, Zola uses the distorted shadow to suggest a supernaturally evil power, a force to which eventually Gervaise succumbs, in a mixture of fascination and loathing: 'Cette sacrée marmite, ronde comme un ventre de chaudronnière grasse, avec son nez qui s'allongeait et se tortillait, lui soufflait un frisson dans les épaules, une peur mêlée d'un désir' (p. 410). The workings of the still and the poison of its 'vitriol' seem animate purposeful forces, ruthlessly accomplishing their deadly work. The vitriol in Coupeau's veins finally kills him and the same force corrupts and destroys Gervaise. Zola's treatment of this social evil may be grounded in fact, statistics and observation, but it is translated into dramatic and horrifying images.

Another important factor in Zola's picture of working-class life is the worker's occupation, most vividly seen here in the steam and heat which inevitably accompany Gervaise's work, and seem to encourage self-indulgence and laziness. It is also at least in part as a result of Coupeau's occupation that he has his accident and succumbs to idleness and drink, but it is also the poison of alcohol circulating in the very air of Paris that encourages his alcoholism. This in turn affects Gervaise, since

it is when Coupeau's drunken vomiting has made the bedroom
uninhabitable that Gervaise at last accepts Lantier's invitation
to share his bed. All the various pressures conspire, and Lantier seems to have the full force of the milieu behind him: 'Une
conspiration sourde, continue, grandissait, poussait lentement
Gervaise, comme si toutes les femmes, autour d'elle, avaient
dû se satisfaire, en lui donnant un amant' (p. 300). It is the
whole of the milieu, the steam of the laundry, the ever-present
temptation of alcohol, the helplessness of individuals in the
great indifference of the city, and the envy and malice of the
neighbourhood that push Gervaise to defeat and degradation.

There is little neighbourliness in this milieu, though the
Goujets and Gervaise herself stand outside the general run of
malice or indifference, and there is a good-natured camarade-
rie amongst the workmen, and even a boisterous joviality seen
at celebrations like the wedding, or Gervaise's big party. Envy
and malice, however, blight even the merriest occasions. Coupeau's sister, Mme Lorilleux, is a mine of petty nastiness,
delighted to be able to spoil Gervaise's wedding-day by giving
her the nickname 'La Banban'. She is so enviously resentful
of Gervaise's setting up her own business that she and her
husband seem to derive positive satisfaction from the setback
of Coupeau's accident. Their malicious triumph at the frustration of her hopes helps to reactivate Gervaise's determination
to get a shop of her own. When Nana runs away from home,
Mme Lorilleux's satisfaction is complete, and she spreads the
vilest slanders about her sister-in-law (p. 423). Gervaise's final
humiliation is a feast for the Lorilleux's self-righteous malevo-
lence. In these mean buildings, the frustrated hopes, endemic
brutality and hopeless ignorance of the inhabitants do not
foster generosity of spirit. As Coupeau prances about on the
roof-top just before his fall, an old woman watches him from
a window, and after his fall, closes her window as if satisfied
(pp. 143-46).

Zola's picture of the slum-dwellers is not a flattering one;
it suggests that their abysmal ignorance and stunted lives encourage a selfish and self-protective brutishness. Coupeau
refuses Goujet's offer to teach him to read during his convales-
cence: he prefers to maintain his lazy illiteracy. The visit of

the wedding-party to the Louvre stresses their 'ignorance ahu-rie' (p. 102); the general bigotry, gullibility and attachment to all sorts of naïve superstitions make a similar point. Grilled mouse is recommended as a cure for intestinal worms (p. 227), and when ways of ensuring the birth of a male child are discussed, Lorilleux maintains that the head of the mother's bed must be turned to the north, while Madame Lerat insists on fresh nettles hidden under the mattress (p. 131). Recom-mended methods of abortion range from a glass of holy water every night, accompanied by three signs of the cross over the womb, to a hard-boiled egg every two hours, and spinach leaves applied to the back (pp. 222-23). We may laugh at such grotesque ideas, but with a shudder that these pitiable notions are all they have. Deprived of education and living from hand to mouth, they inhabit a narrow and bigoted world of preju-dice, superstition and hearsay. In Zola's presentation of the milieu, we have not so much the sense of the characters inha-biting the milieu as of the milieu inhabiting the characters, shaping their lives not merely from without but from within.

iv) THE MILIEU WITHIN

One obvious manifestation of the influence of the milieu working within the characters is in their language. Zola has a great feeling for the *verdeur* of the popular language, and he raided at least two printed sources of contemporary slang[7] to supplement his own experience and observations. He produces in *L'Assommoir* a racy and colloquial style that reflects the vitality of the Parisian working-class idiom – its humour, its irreverent gaiety and even its more violent crudities.

As the Coupeau wedding-party makes its way through the streets, shopkeepers and passers-by joke and laugh at the grotesque array of colours and costumes and the bizarre var-iety of hats. Behind Mme Lorilleux, full of airs and graces in

---

[7] Denis Poulot's *Le Sublime* (1870) and Alfred Delvau's *Dictionnaire de la langue verte* (1866). On these and other sources consulted by Zola, see *Dossier*, pp. 544-45.

her too tight black silk, comes the very pregnant Mme Gaud-
ron who provokes a great deal of gross humour on the lines of
'Tiens, la mariée!' or 'Elle a avalé un rude pépin!' (p. 99), all
of which is met with good-natured laughter. Such humour not
only offers welcome light relief in a novel where so much is
dark, but also helps to show the natural liveliness and capacity
for shared merriment of those for whom life is, most of the
time, no joke. The frequently coarse language of L'Assommoir
aroused considerable disapproval, but without it, Zola could
not have created so vivid an impression of the daily life of the
faubourgs. The range of the language from propriety to vulgarity and obscenity also allows an effective underlining of
changes of mood and attitude in the characters – notably in
Gervaise, who moves from a relative gentility of expression,
when she is still good-naturedly concerned to maintain her
respectability and decency, to a coarse obscenity in her despair.

The early cheerfulness of Coupeau's racy humour also
darkens as the novel progresses. His Parisian verve stands him
in good stead when he and his bride are hustled through the
marriage ceremony: '"Voilà!" dit Coupeau, avec un rire gêné.
Il se dandinait, il ne trouvait rien là de rigolo. Pourtant, il
ajouta: "Ah bien! ça ne traîne pas. Ils vous envoient ça en
quatre mouvements... C'est comme chez les dentistes: on n'a
pas le temps de crier ouf! Ils marient sans douleur"' (pp.
91-92). He enlivens the wedding-feast with a ventriloquism
that makes the stewed rabbit 'miaow' suggestively, and at the
fête, he gaily chaffs Mme Putois when she asks for a glass of
water: 'Est-ce que les honnêtes gens buvaient de l'eau? Elle
voulait donc avoir des grenouilles dans l'estomac?' (p. 261).
It is a long way from this cheerful banter to the cruelty of
his drunken responses to Gervaise later in the novel. When
Gervaise in despair contemplates prostitution, Coupeau encourages her – 'T'es pas encore trop mal, quand tu te débar-
bouilles' – and follows this up with a sardonic proverb: 'Tu
sais, comme on dit, il n'y a pas si vieille marmite qui ne trouve
son couvercle...' (p. 460).

In his preface, Zola points to the linguistic interest of his
novel and the study he has made of 'la langue du peuple': 'ma
volonté était de faire un travail purement philologique, que je

crois d'un vif intérêt historique et social'. Whether it be Lorilleux, the *chaîniste,* working on his *colonnes,* Coupeau the
roofer, Goujet the foundryman or Gervaise the laundress, Zola
gives us the precise vocabulary of the technical processes
which are part of their everyday routine. The technical vocabulary draws us into the interiority – the private language – of
their experience. The 'travail purement philologique' involves
not merely the use of accurate terminology but the importa-
tion of the popular idiom, with its racy and vigorous images,
its grammatical eccentricities and sometimes crude vocabulary, into both the dialogue and the narrative of the novel.

Zola sets out to capture a way of life, a mode of thinking
and feeling, embedded in the language. The images and points
of reference of the Parisian working-class of the epoch initiate
us into the preoccupations of a specific class at a particular
moment in history. Contemporary figures and events colour
the language and the framing of experience, while the immediate conditions of existence – poverty, hardship and ignorance – limit understanding and expectations, and encourage
reliance on a sort of basic cultural code. This code, implicit
in the language, provides a common fund of agreed 'truths'
and values, rules of etiquette, tribal laws, beliefs and customs
and the clichés that provide the common ground of a shared
ethos. Zola's sharp and well-trained ear for the tribal language
allows him to show, with great economy, how the lives of his
characters, their means of expression and their very imagination are shaped by 'le milieu de rude besogne et de misère où
ils vivent' (p. 18).

The very first snatch of conversation in the novel places
the characters in their historical frame, and tells a good deal
about the manners and customs of their class. Seeing Gervaise's tear-stained face and the bed not slept in, Coupeau tries,
good-naturedly, to cheer her up by suggesting that it is Lantier's interest in politics that has kept him out all night: 'Ne
vous désolez pas, madame Lantier. Il s'occupe beaucoup de
politique; l'autre jour, quand on a voté pour Eugène Sue, un
bon, paraît-il, il était comme un fou. Peut-être bien qu'il a
passé la nuit avec des amis à dire du mal de cette crapule de
Bonaparte' (p. 22). The 'paraît-il' clearly indicates the vague

hearsay that underpins Coupeau's estimation of Sue, and the 'peut-être bien' indicates the optimistic goodwill that inspires his explanation of Lantier's absence, while 'cette crapule de Bonaparte' incisively if inelegantly indicates the current villain of the political stage. Gervaise answers not what he has actually said, but what his words have implied. 'Non, non, murmura-t-elle avec effort, ce n'est pas ce que vous croyez. Je sais où est Lantier...' (p. 22). And Coupeau in turn responds not to what she says but to what he understands: 'Coupeau cligna les yeux, pour montrer qu'il n'était pas dupe de ce mensonge'. In this milieu, there is little privacy, and Lantier's conduct is not at all exceptional. It is easy for Coupeau to read the situation, and Gervaise knows it. Etiquette demands, however, that their exchanges observe the social conventions. Language, for the inarticulate, is often more a shelter than a means of expression, but the truth of the situation has been seized by both parties, and before he leaves, Coupeau assures Gervaise that she can count on him 'le jour où elle serait dans la peine' (p. 22).

Clichés and commonplaces often come into play to protect very dubious modes of conduct, as when Coupeau enthusiastically defends his friendship with Lantier, lending it a spurious aura of folk-wisdom by appeal to an accepted notion of male solidarity. Lantier is, he maintains, 'un bougre à poils... Enfin, ils se comprenaient, ils étaient bâtis l'un pour l'autre. L'amitié avec un homme, c'est plus solide que l'amour avec une femme' (p. 307). Later, Coupeau invokes conventional notions of family honour when denouncing Nana's conduct, despite the ludicrousness of such pretensions (p. 430). Nana's misbehaviour is itself covered by another piece of folk wisdom, in which 'toutes les fleuristes tournaient mal' (p. 437), and if Lantier continues to thrive, while wrecking the lives of others, 'il n'y a que les hommes de cette espèce qui aient de la chance' (p. 378). There are accepted 'truths' for every occasion. Too much drinking may be bad, but 'le vin nourrit l'ouvrier' (p. 232). A code of accepted conduct is enshrined in clichés and proverbs that express the conventions, expectations and norms of the society.

Zola brings out the unwritten propositions underlying the language of the *faubourgs*: rivalries, family crises, alliances all have their appropriate attitudes and approved phrases. It is in part Goujet's failure to respect the tribal norms that undermines his attempt to persuade Gervaise to run off with him to Belgium. It is not that adultery is impossible, far from it, but Goujet moves outside the conventions. Gervaise's reaction to his suggestion that they go away together is striking: 'Alors, elle devint très rouge. Il l'aurait prise contre lui pour l'embrasser, qu'elle aurait eu moins de honte' (p. 305). She is alarmed at the strangeness of his offer; his language and behaviour seem inappropriate and unreal, like something in a novel: 'C'était un drôle de garçon tout de même, de lui proposer un enlèvement, comme cela se passe dans les romans et dans la haute société'. Gervaise's conventions are quite other: 'Ah bien! autour d'elle, elle voyait des ouvriers faire la cour à des femmes mariées; mais ils ne les menaient pas même à Saint-Denis, ça se passait sur place, et carrément' (p. 305). Her earthy sense of reality is baffled. Zola makes it clear that Gervaise is more accustomed to succumbing under pressure than to assuming responsibility for freely-made choices: confused, she falls back on the conventionally pious sentiments appropriate to the 'honnête femme': 'Ce n'est pas possible, monsieur Goujet. Ce serait très mal... Je suis mariée, n'est-ce pas? J'ai des enfants...'; ending with a comment that seems in retrospect bitterly ironic: 'quand on reste honnête, dans notre position, on est joliment récompensé' (p. 306).

The incident is telling in its revelation of the norms that underlie their conduct and their words. Goujet's unconventional offer paradoxically elicits from Gervaise, after some initial stammering, a retreat into the tribal shelter of her role as wife and mother, and Goujet then acquiesces in the conventions: 'Il hochait la tête en l'écoutant. Il l'approuvait, il ne pouvait pas dire le contraire' (p. 306). He kisses her, crushing her briefly with the force of his pent-up passion, and lets her go. Despite this one passionate kiss, it is the *lieux communs* of accepted morality that triumph in this scene. The *lieu commun* has, as Sartre shrewdly comments, 'plusieurs sens: il désigne sans doute les pensées les plus rebattues mais c'est que

ces pensées sont devenues le lieu de rencontre de la commu-
nauté. Chacun s'y retrouve, y retrouve les autres'.[8] By showing
the gap between Gervaise's spontaneous response (the amusement and the edge of mockery in 'C'était un drôle de garçon
tout de même') and the moral clichés of her spoken words,
Zola points simultaneously to the gulf and to the common
ground between Goujet and Gervaise. Gervaise's inner reactions reflect the practice of the milieu while her words utter
its pious conventions: Goujet's words, on the other hand, try
briefly to move away from the conventions to a more pragma-
tic and personal view which, however, he inwardly feels to be
wrong. The exercise of choice, initiated by Goujet, is inhibited
by tribal taboo and by a sense of abnormality that robs Goujet's project of reality.

The Lorilleux couple embody some of the ugliest inward
operations of the milieu. They turn away the starving Gervaise
without a *sou* or a crust, but with the standard declaration: 'Le
cœur y est toujours... Seulement, quand on ne peut pas, on
ne peut pas' (p. 468). Mme Lorilleux is particularly obnoxious
in her incessant self-righteousness, meanness and malice; but
she always has a sharp sense of what is 'proper'. Christening
presents are bought to keep up appearances, public tributes
and gestures are made, however reluctantly. The hypocrisy of
the Lorilleux earns them full membership in their society.
Gervaise's generosity, just as much as her failings, flouts the
rules. When we compare the situations of Gervaise and the
Lorilleux at the end, we can see some justification for their
stringent economy, if not for their dedicated meanness. The
Lorilleux are proved 'right' by the fact of their survival. From
the Lorilleux viewpoint, Gervaise was wrong to keep Coupeau
at home when she might have sent him to the hospital, and
wrong again to rent her shop on borrowed money, wrong to
borrow money for Maman Coupeau's funeral, wrong to spend
so much on her *fête*. But heart for heart, there is no compari-
son between Gervaise and her in-laws, who so impeccably
enact the tribal imperatives of self-protection and survival.

[8] Sartre, J.-P., préface, in Nathalie Sarraute, *Portrait d'un inconnu,* Paris,
Gallimard, 1956.

v) GERVAISE'S *FÊTE*

Gervaise's *fête* is a pivotal episode in Zola's presentation of the milieu, and it marks a turning-point in the fortunes of the laundry and the Coupeau family. Many different elements of Zola's narrative skill here work closely together to great effect: his eye for the physical details, the language and the customs of the *quartier,* his skill in the management of groups of people, his characterization and the artful patterning by which he gives extension and intensity to events. Standing at the centre of the novel, the *fête* provides a dramatic focus for many diverse elements of the environment and a hub for the thematic patterns of the novel.

As well as being a personal celebration (Gervaise's saint's-day, June 19), the *fête* comes as the culmination of a communal desire which builds up for weeks before the feast takes place: 'On cherchait des plats, on s'en léchait les lèvres. Toute la boutique avait une sacrée envie de nocer. Il fallait une rigolade à la mort' (p. 236). The 'on', the 'toute la boutique' and the impersonal 'il fallait' underline the communal involvement and the songs and recitations that follow the banquet are an expression of the spirit and the vigorous oral traditions of the *faubourg.* The extravagance of the feast is itself a response to the resentment which success provokes in the social group, and a defiance, through recklessness and prodigality, of the constrictions – the prudence and thrift – of a life always on the edge of penury. It is also a gesture of exasperation at a situation in which all the fruits of work and effort are being frittered away in drink – 'Puisque l'argent filait quand même, autant valait-il faire gagner au boucher qu'au marchand de vin' (p. 236).

As Gervaise and Maman Coupeau prepare the table for the guests, realistic details acquire a symbolic thrust. The conversion of the work-table into a dining-table for the banquet points up the feast's dismantling of the working structure of the laundry, and this is further sharpened by the arrival of an angry, dissatisfied customer to whom Gervaise makes lying excuses with an already practised ease. The recklessness of

Gervaise's pursuit of her aim is evident when, discovering she has run out of money, she falls back on a resource of long ago – the pawn-shop. 'Etait-elle bête! elle n'y songeait plus' (p. 242) is her immediate reflection, which, transcribed, as it were, directly from her thoughts, shows the naïve, unthinking joy of solving the immediate problem, without any sense of the enormity of this return to a way of life long happily left behind. In her satisfaction at this forgotten resource, Gervaise quickly adds a significant item to the black silk dress destined for the pawnbroker – her wedding-ring.

The preparations for the feast demonstrate dramatically the dissolution of Gervaise's honesty and pride in her work, the crumbling of her marriage and her integrity, the loss of her scruples and her capitulation to the imperatives of gluttony and vengeful triumph. The contrast between surface and underlying realities is heightened by the initial Sunday-best gentility of the laundry assistants, and by the pretensions of Virginie, who arrives 'mise comme une dame... avec une écharpe et un chapeau, bien qu'elle eût eu seulement la rue à traverser' (p. 245). In the suffocating heat of the kitchen, into which the women crowd, a dress catches briefly on the roasting-pan, and the cooking-smells mingle with the scent of the flowers brought for Gervaise, as 'les dames' pin up their skirts to keep them clean. Meanwhile Boche is already asking Clémence whether she's ticklish, producing gales of laughter from the suggestible laundress: 'On riait, on en lâchait de fortes' (p. 246).

Jollity is poised precariously on the edge of lewdness, and threatened by the hovering presence of Lantier; the absence of Mme Goujet, supposedly because of her sciatica, seems an inevitable and meaningful token of her disapproval. The shadow cast by the figure of Lantier lengthens when Gervaise realizes that without Mme Goujet they will be thirteen at table. The superstitions of the milieu underline the sense of foreboding as Gervaise announces '"Nous sommes treize!", ... voyant là une nouvelle preuve du malheur dont elle se sentait menacée depuis quelque temps' (p. 252). Throughout this chapter, that sense of menace accumulates.

The party gets under way, and steadily works its way through the courses. By the time the goose arrives, the 'clarté pâle' of the twilight filtered through the muslin-draped windows has given way to 'un jour sale, d'un gris de cendre' (p. 256) and the newly-lit lamps light up wine-stains and débris, greasy plates and sweating faces. As Gervaise recites a litany of impressive facts about the goose, Virginie interrupts to insist on how wonderful it looked even when raw: 'on l'aurait mangée comme ça, disait-elle, tant la peau était fine et blanche, une peau de blonde, quoi!' (p. 257). The 'peau de blonde' is a suggestive phrase, echoing as it does the 'beaux bras de blonde' (p. 34) of Gervaise. By the description of the table as 'une chapelle' (p. 243) and the attribution of the 'peau de blonde' to the goose, the narrative evokes, beneath the recounting of immediate events, deeper patterns of suggestion, in which the table of the banquet seems an altar on which Gervaise herself will be carved up and devoured.

As the feast goes on, efforts at refinement give way to the simple indulgence of gluttony and the relaxed manners of drunkenness. The pseudo-formality with which Mme Lerat proposes the appointment of Poisson 'qui a l'usage des armes' as carver (p. 258), is offset by the coarseness of Boche who, seeing a spurt of juice from the goose, comments: 'Moi, je m'abonne... pour qu'on me fasse comme ça pipi dans la bouche' (p. 259) which provokes cries of disgust from the ladies and a severe reprimand from Mme Boche, mortified by her husband's lack of decency. Second-hand opinions and semi-genteel civilities alternate with greedy gobblings and coarseness of speech and gesture. Mme Lerat's rather specialized verbal sensitivity sniffs out salacious innuendos in the most innocuous-seeming remarks, and Clémence guffaws with laughter at the indecent whispering of Boche; the children scream at each other in the kitchen; Boche strokes Mme Vigouroux's knee under the table, and the surface proprieties are eroded by a progressive abandon to the satisfaction of animal appetites.

When the doors are opened to the street, the whole neighbourhood is involved in the feast, and passing coachmen add their gross jocularities to the scene – '"Ohé! la grosse mère, je vas chercher l'accoucheuse!..."' (p. 263) and so forth. Even as the festivity spreads outwards in a wave of bonhomie and indulgence, jealousy and envy are also seething beneath the surface. When Lorilleux notices that the dining-table is the work-top that usually serves for the ironing, he makes the most of it: ' "mais c'est sur votre établi que nous mangeons! Ah bien! on n'a peut-être jamais autant travaillé dessus!" Cette plaisanterie méchante', the narrative comments, 'eut un grand succès' (p. 267). The guests develop the joke: the cream cheese tastes of starch, says Mme Lerat, while Mme Lorilleux mutters between clenched teeth about the folly of eating away one's money on the very boards on which it was earned.

Jocularity and malice, civility and crass vulgarity sit cheek by jowl in this celebration where Gervaise reaches the high point of her triumph in – and over – the neighbourhood. But it is clear that even within the circle of family and friends gathered at the table, the feast is highly ambivalent – an act of generosity or of foolish and overweening pride, an occasion for affection or for hate and envy. Viewing it retrospectively, the reader can see it as both an apogee and the beginning of a cruel fall, in which inherent weakness joins forces with external pressures to bear Gervaise to destruction.

With the songs, Zola allows the popular voice to invade the text, not here as an element assimilated into his own narrative form but as an extrinsic element, framed in its own forms. The songs add variety, colour and humour as well as an extra touch of authenticity, and Zola also interweaves their themes with the characters and themes of the novel. The main subjects of these popular and often vulgar songs are sex and drink, and although the songs' origins lie outside the immediate world of the feast, they are very much part of the traditions of this society. Many of the songs reflect the singer and have reverberations far beyond the present scene. Gervaise, for instance, reluctantly offers 'Ah! laissez-moi dormir', and when the words speak longingly of a sleep full of beautiful dreams, her eye-lids half-close (p. 269). That longing for sleep expresses her desire to close her eyes to the realities of her life, and it will be echoed later in the novel by her yearning to 'dormir un mois, surtout en hiver, le mois du terme' (p. 389). This in turn ultimately becomes a longing for death as the last means of escape.

Poisson, predictably, sings a patriotic song; then some exotic love-songs bring dreams of a far-away world to this assembly starved of luxury and romance. Bru, bereft of memory, and in 'une voix caverneuse', repeats, over and over, the same two lines, in which the only identifiable word is 'trou':

> Trou la la, trou la la,
> Trou la, trou la, trou la la! (p. 271)

Brought in to stave off the bad luck of thirteen, Bru turns into an unwitting prophet of doom. His lugubrious song is interrupted by Virginie, who points out that Lantier is now standing outside, looking at them. It is not merely its association with the arrival of Lantier and with talk of a hanged woman (p. 272) that makes Bru's strange song seem so doom-laden. The resonance of Bru's 'trou la la' comes from the beginning of the novel and continues to the end, mingling suggestively with Gervaise's *idéal*, in which the word 'trou' figures prominently.[9]

Gervaise first articulates her *idéal* to Coupeau as 'de travailler tranquille, de manger toujours du pain, d'avoir un trou un peu propre pour dormir' (p. 61), and it is recalled at intervals throughout the novel. It recurs, for instance, when a jubilant Gervaise feels she has more than fulfilled her early and very modest ambitions: 'travailler, manger du pain, avoir un trou à soi, élever ses enfants, ne pas être battue, mourir dans son lit. Et maintenant son idéal était dépassé...' (p. 170). Bru himself lives (and dies) in a sort of understairs cupboard frequently referred to as his 'trou' (see pp. 387, 517). The very name 'Bru' (daughter-in-law) suggests a link with Gervaise (the only daughter-in-law in the Coupeau family), and a further link is suggested through their work. Gervaise is a 'blanchisseuse', and Bru, who describes himself as having spent half a century 'à peindre des portes et à *blanchir des plafonds* aux quatre coins de Paris' (p. 229; my italics), can be seen as a sort of 'blanchisseur'. And it is Gervaise who, after the death of Bru, occupies his hole, and like him, dies in it. Viewed in the

---

[9] Jacques Dubois comments on 'trou' as a key-word, in *23*, p. 51.

wider context of the novel, Bru's doleful song seems a mocking
echo and a predictive dirge.

Mme Lerat offers a sad and sentimental ballad called 'L'Enfant du Bon Dieu'. Gervaise, tormented by the hovering figure
of Lantier, identifies with 'cette enfant perdue, abandonnée'
and gives way to tears. Her tears are, with hindsight, well
justified, for Coupeau is just about to bring Lantier into the
household. The celebration ends in an explosion of noise, and
no-one has any clear and distinct memory of what happened,
save that Clémence became totally indecent and was sick over
the curtains, while the men at least went outside – a mark of
their good manners, in the tribal view. The party breaks up to
the accompaniment of a furious quarrel between the Lorilleux
and a repeat of the ' "'trou la la" entêté et lugubre du père Bru'.
Zola's narrative here reproduces the confusion of the end
of the evening, with uncertain and fragmentary memories,
among which we find Gervaise's impression that Goujet was
sobbing as he left, and a vague memory of warm breath in her
hair – but whether from Lantier or the night air, she does not
know. The chapter ends with a final victorious incursion from
the milieu, when a neighbour's cat steals in and finishes off
the blonde-skinned goose, crunching the bones 'avec le petit
bruit de ses dents fines' (p. 280).

In this central scene, Zola brings all the characters of the
novel together and captures the accents and tricks of speech,
the habitual gestures and attitudes of the *quartier,* the shifting
moods, the common culture, the alliances and resentments,
the joviality and the despair. The 'realist' representation of
reality becomes deeply symbolic as observed details acquire
semantic weight in the frame of Zola's vision.

2

Figures in the Web

L I K E poetry, in Mallarmé's well-known phrase, characters are made with words. The words in which Zola outlines his fictional creations and endows them with convincing vitality are selected and ordered by thought, feeling and art. From their beginnings in the *Ebauches*, Zola's characters have specific roles to play in his design: as he inscribes them into the chosen framework – here the 'faubourgs empestés' – they acquire the particularity which allows them to animate it by their interaction with it, and to impose upon the reader a sense of their living presence.

i) METHODS OF PRESENTATION

Some essential elements of Zola's presentation of his very large cast of characters can be seen in miniature in his treatment of the streams of workers pouring into Paris in the early morning. At times they form an indeterminate mass – an impressionistic blur: 'Cette foule, de loin, gardait un effacement plâtreux, un ton neutre, où le bleu déteint et le gris sale dominaient' (p. 22). The distanced view alternates with brief close-ups, when the eye differentiates the different trades – 'On reconnaissait les serruriers à leurs bourgerons bleus, les maçons à leurs cottes blanches...' (p. 22) – and individual movements are picked out: a worker stops to relight his pipe, men disappear into bars, where the shutters are just coming down. The techniques used here exemplify the way Zola makes his characters known to the reader, relating them first to their milieu, then identifying them by name and occupation and pinpointing salient features of their physical appearance, costume, voice, gestures, or mannerisms. These techniques also illustrate the shifts of focus Zola makes throughout the novel, alternating 'wide-screen' shots of crowds with close-up shots of groups or individuals.

The description of the wedding-party similarly combines striking vignettes of individuals – like Mme Lerat 'fagotée dans une robe puce trop large dont les longs effilés la faisaient ressembler à un caniche maigre sortant de l'eau' (p. 93) – with a collective view of 'la noce' trailing through the streets like a multi-coloured caterpillar. Treating it as a single entity, Zola creates delightfully bizarre impressions, often with splendidly comic effect, as in the Louvre: 'quand la noce se fut engagée dans le musée assyrien, elle eut un petit frisson' (pp. 99-100).

In the opening chapter, Zola not only introduces Gervaise, but two major characters, Lantier and Coupeau, and two others, Mme Boche and Virginie, who, although minor, play important roles in the novel. Mme Boche is the first to appear, at first simply as 'une grosse femme, nu-tête, en tablier' (p. 23). Her name is given to us by Gervaise, and a very rapid authorial intervention explains that she is the concierge of a nearby building. Her occupation alternates with her name as a means of designation, effectively underlining the inquisitive-ness (traditionally associated with her occupation) that domin-ates in her encounter with Gervaise. In the *lavoir* scene, Mme Boche takes shape as a woman who, despite moments of apparent kindness and concern, is an avid scandal-monger. Her show of sympathy is undermined by a sudden sharp view of her face which reveals her inflamed excitement: 'Sa bouche était à demi ouverte dans sa grosse face; ses yeux, à fleur de tête, luisaient' (p. 35). As well as etching this strong visual image, Zola here uses a revealing 'overview' to supplement snatches of conversation with tell-tale fragments of unspoken thoughts which give depth to his portrait, showing how in-stinctive movements of human sympathy in Mme Boche are counterbalanced by an over-riding passion for gossip. Virginie, sister of the *brunisseuse,* Adèle,[10] with whom Lantier runs off, is a dressmaker who lodges in the apartments presided over by

[10] Zola here suggestively contrasts 'brunisseuse' and 'blanchisseuse'.

Mme Boche. About the same age as Gervaise, she is slightly taller, dark and pretty. Her vanity is indicated by the coquettish red ribbon round her neck and the provocative bravado with which she swings her hips as she goes by in the wash-house. In the fight that follows, Gervaise publicly humiliates her rival's sister, and creates, as becomes evident in the later part of the novel, an enemy for life. There is no danger, after the wash-house battle, of the reader's forgetting who Virginie is.

Coupeau is the first of the major characters to enter Gervaise's world, and he does so as 'une voix jeune et gaie', identified as 'Monsieur Coupeau' by Gervaise, and described in a short explanatory paragraph as 'un ouvrier zingueur qui occupait, tout en haut de l'hôtel, un cabinet de dix francs. Il avait son sac passé à l'épaule...' (p. 21). His situation, work and sympathetic attitude to Gervaise are rapidly sketched, and we are left with a simple and rather jaunty outline of a good-natured and friendly fellow, with his toolbag slung over his shoulder. This initial sketch, with its hints of Coupeau's interest in Gervaise, and indications, in his comradely efforts to provide excuses for Lantier, of a sort of instinctive male solidarity, creates a useful platform for his future development.

Lantier, whose entrance (like that of Virginie) is also his exit for several chapters, must, to sustain his role as a major actor in this drama (even when off-stage), make a distinct impression in this first scene. His entrance is carefully prepared and comes after the conversations with Coupeau and Mme Boche, in both of which he is the subject of conversation. He makes his entrance 'tranquillement', in deliberate contrast to the anxiety with which he is awaited. His prickly rejection of Gervaise's concern is immediately striking. To her cry of 'C'est toi! c'est toi!' he responds with an icy 'Oui, c'est moi. Après? ...Tu ne vas pas commencer tes bêtises, peut-être!' (p. 25). Pushing her aside, he tosses his hat away from him with an ill-tempered gesture that reflects his unspoken desire to toss away with equal ease his obligation to her and the two children. After this telling gesture, Zola gives a rapid pen-picture of Lantier – his stocky figure and good looks, the moustache he has the habit of curling round his fingers, and his strong Provençal accent. The picture gives the essentials of Lantier:

his vanity and his pleasure-seeking egoism. Before he leaves,
Lantier helps himself to the sole remaining money. The scene
is prophetic of the way Lantier will parasitically use people
until there is nothing more to be got out of them, then turn
away contemptuously to look for a new host.

As more and more characters are assimilated into the
novel, names, nicknames, trades and descriptive tags ('ce lou-
chon d'Augustine', 'la grande Clémence') help to keep them
clearly identified.[11] Sometimes the name itself operates almost
as a nickname, as with the *Lor*illeux, whose name recalls *l'or*
with which they work or Poisson, to whom Virginie is carrying
his favourite dish (a fresh mackerel!)[12] when his name first
appears. Coupeau's name, 'coupe-eau', can be seen as reflecting both his addiction to alcohol and his roofer's trade of
keeping out water. Nicknames add a picturesque element to
the identification of minor characters like Mes-Bottes or Bec-
Salé, or highlight specific features. 'La Banban' insists on
Gervaise's lameness, while 'la Gueule d'Or' focuses attention
on Goujet's golden beard and heroic quality. Trades provide
a convenient variation on the names – Lantier ('le chapelier'),
Goujet ('le forgeron'), Gervaise ('la blanchisseuse') or Bazouge
('le croque-mort)' – and often serve as useful reminders, as
when Coupeau re-enters the story in Chapter II as 'Coupeau,
l'ouvrier zingueur'.

To help familiarize the reader with the characters, Zola
often prepares the way for them. Mes-Bottes, for instance, is
briefly seen in 'L'Assommoir' before he appears at the wedding celebrations. Coupeau's family is also described beforehand
so that the relationships – and occupations – of the various
family members are known before we meet them. Such
preparations could involve very awkward passages of exposition, but Zola introduces them with plausible naturalness after
the 'prune' at the 'Assommoir', when Gervaise walks with
Coupeau to the apartment-block (p. 6). When Gervaise is
taken to meet the Lorilleux, the names on the doors of the

[11] These tags and labels are discussed in Chapter II of *17*.
[12] Philippe Hamon (*27*, p. 130) points out the ironic word-play of Virginie
'si peu vierge' and her 'maquereau' – the slang word for a pimp.

various apartments provide an early introduction to some of the inhabitants (pp. 74-75), who will later become familiar figures in Gervaise's daily life. Vivid visual images also help to fix characters in the reader's mind and give them a certain emotional coloration. Madame Goujet's black dress underlines her gravity; Mme Lerat's bean-pole figure – 'sèche comme un échalas' (p. 110) – and blameless life make an effective contrast for her obsessive interest in sexual matters and her mania for suggestive innuendos. The hypocritical bonhomie of M. Marescot, the owner of the apartment-block, who treats his tenants with cold ruthlessness, is made apparent in brief but insistent references to his huge hands (see pp. 159, 161, 357, 384).

The darker, instinctual side of humanity is often suggested by images that link human and animal behaviour.[13] The hidden lust for vengeance in Virginie is pinpointed in the cat-like 'étincelles jaunes' (p. 224) which Gervaise seems to perceive in her dark eyes when the two women meet again and apparently decide to let bygones be bygones. The image recurs many times (see, for instance, pp. 347, 441). In Gervaise herself we see a gradual infiltration of animality as her humanity and individuality are progressively reduced. She begins to be 'gloutonne comme une chatte' (p. 260); she is cat-like too in her attachment to the comfort of Lantier's clean sheets (p. 329), and when she owes money in every direction and has lost both dignity and hope, 'elle se secouait comme un chien battu' (p. 338). Coupeau and Lantier, allies in debauchery, are presented in a similar way: 'ils se frottaient l'un contre l'autre toute la journée, comme les chats qui cherchent et cultivent leur plaisir' (p. 342), and the Lorilleux, exulting in Gervaise's downfall, are described as purring 'comme des matous qu'on caresse' (p. 404).

The characters are, above all, mediators between author and reader, figures through whose eyes, ears and feelings the reader makes a focused and 'living' contact with a specific

---

[13] See Philippe Bonnefis's study of Zola's animal imagery in 'Le Bestiaire d'Emile Zola' in *26* (also in *13*, pp. 117-28).

world anchored in time and space by a mass of accurately observed detail. Without the characters, the framework and its load of information on language, trades, customs and conditions would be no more, in novelistic terms, than dead weight. The great risk of an enterprise such as Zola's is that the human figures will be dwarfed by the frame and lost in an overcrowded canvas. It has indeed often been objected to Zola that his concern is more with the mass than the individual, and that his characters, in consequence, do not create the impression of reality associated with psychological depth and complexity.

From a different standpoint, however, Zola's supposed neglect of individual characterization has been seen as a positive attribute in tune with a modernist anti-characterizing aesthetic. Philippe Hamon, for instance, comments appreciatively on 'cette "disparition" du personnage de roman chez Zola derrière le faisceau des corrélations et des influences qui le déterminent' (*27*, p. 25). In my own view, Zola's characters, despite the lack of psychological analysis, do not disappear at all. Far from it. The central characters are vividly, physically and emotionally present, and if their words, thoughts and feelings are, on the whole, expressed without apparent complexity or subtlety, the novelist weaves them into a network of references, images and associations that gives them an astonishing richness and depth. Zola seems to create his characters from within, by the force of his imaginative empathy, seeing and feeling from their perspective and in their terms, as they encounter a world based in observed reality but infused, shaped and coloured by his vision. If Zola's stupendous efforts at exhaustive and accurate representation of reality provide a wide panorama of objectively verifiable detail, it is his own vision that selects and structures the elements of that world (see *33*, pp. 71-74) into a stage on which to dramatize the conscious and unconscious impulses that govern his own manner of seeing, and his sense of the comic and tragic, the irony, cruelty and beauty of life.

ii) GERVAISE

Zola's attachment to the individual figure caught in the mesh of reality is everywhere evident and everywhere vital. Zola is undoubtedly concerned with the mass, and he does indeed select 'sample' figures to illustrate his perceptions and observations of the greater masses, but these figures become a vivid focus for the interaction between the individual and the surrounding world. Gervaise is such a 'sample' figure, but, far from observing her dispassionately as a representative of her class, Zola introduces her in a highly emotional scene that immediately enlists our sympathies and draws us gradually but insistently more and more into her mind and feelings, so that she becomes the eyes through which we view her world, and Zola's voice blends into hers for much of the narrative. This Gervaise/Zola voice makes even explanatory interpolations blend into the narrative without any jarring change of tone. The narrative 'overview', for instance, which tells us: 'Au fond, Gervaise ne se sentait pas devant Lantier si courageuse qu'elle le disait' merges into an 'underview' as the narration moves into that 'fond', as if articulating Gervaise's own reflections: 'Certes, elle était bien résolue à ne pas lui permettre de la toucher seulement du bout des doigts' (p. 306). Even more striking is the fusion of Gervaise's voice with the voice that controls the chronology of the novel, as in the opening of Chapter XII – 'Ce devait être le samedi après le terme, quelque chose comme le 12 ou le 13 janvier, Gervaise ne savait plus au juste. Elle perdait la boule...' (p. 461).[14]

By focusing our attention, from the start, on the central figure of Gervaise, Zola is able to radiate outwards, locating all the characters within her world, and making effective use of a system of tags or reminders to fix them in the reader's mind. Gervaise provides the unifying consciousness through which the characters and events of the novel are related. The impact of events is heightened by their being registered from Gervaise's viewpoint and in terms that relate them very closely

---

[14] For a searching analysis of Zola's use of the narrative voice, in conjunction with the 'discours indirect libre', see *23*, pp. 131-87.

to Gervaise's experience – we hear the terrible thud of Coupeau's fall with the ears of the laundress – it is 'le coup sourd d'un paquet de linge jeté de haut' (p. 146). We see Coupeau drunkenly swaying, 'avec un mouvement de balancier d'horloge' (p. 175), and hear him snoring 'avec la régularité d'un tic-tac énorme d'horloge' (p. 185) in terms that derive from Gervaise's fascination with the clocks in the shop across the street (p. 168), and the clock-work imagery points to the gulf growing up between Gervaise and the drunken husband who begins to seem more machine than human being. [15]

The novel was originally intended to bear the title 'La Simple Vie de Gervaise Macquart', and Zola refers to the novel familiarly in his notes as 'le roman de Gervaise'. When he changed the title to *L'Assommoir,* he gave the title role to the persecutor rather than the victim. And yet that title, evoking not only Colombe's bar but all the forces by which Gervaise is 'assommée', does not turn our attention away from her, nor reduce her significance, but makes everything and everyone, in the animate and inanimate world about her, lively players in *her* drama.

Complexity of character and psychological analysis, as such, have little place. Gervaise is not capable of searching self-analysis, nor can she articulate her longings and disappointments save on a rather primitive level. There is clearly a risk for the novelist in using so limited a character, with so narrow a range of reflection, at the centre of so grand a play of forces and people. It is a measure of Zola's greatness, his imaginative power, and his compassion, that he succeeds in conveying the rich humanity of Gervaise, involving the reader deeply in her often inarticulate emotions. I stress compassion here since without it Zola could not have the extraordinary, intuitive perception that uncovers, beneath banal words and simple gestures, those profoundly human emotions that are inelegantly but expressively called 'gut-feelings'. We are made so deeply aware of Gervaise's intuitive, instinctive gut-reactions to her life, that we are powerfully moved by the way in which she is gradually dehumanized, sapped of identity and

---

[15] On Zola's 'mechanization' of the human body, see *19,* pp. 215-28.

will, to become, at last, no more than a decomposing object, to be erased from an indifferent universe. There is ultimately a dissolution of Gervaise's individual character, but the reader has been so effectively persuaded of the reality and importance of the human identity which is finally engulfed that this is experienced as a tragic process. Tragic, not tearful. It is not pathos that animates the end of Gervaise and the novel, but something more akin to tragic horror.

Changes in Gervaise's fortunes and character are mapped in spatial terms by her changes of domicile (from the Plassans of her past to the Hotel Boncœur, the rue Neuve, the *boutique* in the rue de la Goutte-d'Or, to the top of the building and finally the 'trou' where she dies), and in emotional terms by changes in her relationships with people (Lantier, Coupeau, Goujet, Madame Goujet, Lalie, Bazouge and Bru, for instance), and things (her beloved clock, her shop, the still of 'L'Assommoir', the apartment block), all highlighted in specific episodes that mark off the stages of her life. And through all the vicissitudes of her life, Zola keeps the reader's sympathy firmly with his heroine.

Gervaise – and the novel opens with the familiarity of her first name – is presented to us in tears and desolation in the opening scene, where already we *see her seeing*. The reader's focus is adjusted to a double lens – an overview in which we see Gervaise's movements and gestures, and the view through her eyes as she gazes out of the window, surveys the bleak room, and returns, barefoot, to the window. When she leaves the window, in reponse to Coupeau's voice, the perspective shifts to Coupeau, through whose eyes we see her face reddened by tears, and learn that she is, for him, 'une belle et brave femme' (p. 22). When Lantier returns, we learn that she is twenty-two, tall, rather slim, with delicate features, but that trailing about in the squalid room, with her hair uncombed and her face distorted by misery, she looks ten years older. Through Lantier's hostile eyes, we first see her lameness, particularly visible that morning after her night of anguish. Lantier, newly enamoured of Adèle, contemplates Gervaise's body with disdain (p. 28), but later, through the gaze of Mme Boche in the wash-house, we see 'Gervaise, les manches re-

troussées, montrant ses beaux bras de blonde, jeunes encore,
à peine rosés aux coudes...' (p. 34). In the fight with Virginie,
a quite different picture emerges – 'Elle avait un visage si terrible, que personne n'osa approcher' (p. 48) – while Coupeau,
during his courtship, sees 'la jeune femme, dont le joli visage
de blonde avait, ce jour-là, une transparence laiteuse de fine
porcelaine' (p. 53). The reader's impressions of Gervaise are
built up from such diverse visual images which change with
the observer, and they are enriched by what Gervaise says
about herself.

Without being introspective and analytical, Gervaise is
aware of many features of her character. Stressing her practica-
lity, her capacity for hard work and her relative indifference
to sexual temptation, she acknowledges her resemblance to her
mother, and her one great weakness – 'd'être très sensible,
d'aimer tout le monde, de se passionner pour des gens qui lui
faisaient ensuite mille misères' (p. 57). That capacity for devotion will be shown abundantly in her early life with Coupeau,
as will, in the course of the novel, the heritage and habit of
submission. Deeper insights into Gervaise's character are offered by her thoughts and feelings, recorded in the narrative by
the use of 'discours indirect libre' – that is, by relating things
and events from her viewpoint, without any accompanying
'she thought' or 'she felt'. Zola gives us Gervaise's view of
things in terms available to her (allowing himself occasionally
and unobtrusively to heighten the language). We thus learn a
great deal about Gervaise from the way that she sees things,
and her inward responses – she is no intellectual, but she is far
from stupid. One of the things that helps to consolidate the
reader's sympathy and respect is, indeed, the intelligent per-
ceptiveness of Gervaise's reactions to the world. Her assess-
ment of Lantier, although belated, is clear and succinct: 'un
ambitieux, un dépensier, un homme qui ne songe qu'à son
amusement. Il ne vaut pas grand-chose' (p. 35). Her first
reactions to Coupeau show a balanced prudence, and her
refusal of him is made 'sans colère, avec une grande sagesse,
très froide... On voyait qu'elle avait arrêté ça dans sa tête, après
de mûres réflexions' (p. 54). When she finally succumbs to
Coupeau's insistence, we recognize the truth of her own self-

appraisal – 'elle se laissait aller où on la poussait, par crainte
de causer de la peine à quelqu'un' (p. 68).

Her reactions to the water from the dyers' shop reflect the
ups and downs of her inner life. The colours change from
pastel shades to muddy brown and black, and while the early
colours seem to mirror the gaiety and hopefulness of the young
Gervaise, there comes a moment when she is no longer in tune
with the pretty tints. Looking down one day, from her high
and tiny room, and remembering herself standing in the courtyard looking up, thirteen years before, she notices a pool of
blue water from the dyers', 'd'un bleu aussi tendre que le bleu
de jadis'. But, she reflects, 'elle, à cette heure, se sentait joliment changée et décatie' (p. 372). After the last disastrous
meeting with Goujet, after, indeed, the destruction of all her
hopes, she sees a black stream flowing into the surrounding
snow, and reflects: 'C'était une eau couleur de ses pensées.
Elles avaient coulé, les belles eaux bleu tendre et rose tendre!'
(p. 495).

It very quickly becomes obvious that Gervaise is a finer
register of experience than, say, Coupeau, or indeed, most of
the other characters. This is no doubt partly because Zola's
narrative gives the reader privileged access to Gervaise's memories, inward reactions and reflections, but it is also due to
the emotional and moral sensitivity with which Zola has en-
dowed her. It is neither complex nor analytical, but womanly
and intuitive. She is quick to perceive, and to be disturbed by,
the gap between the bravado of Coupeau's private condemnations of the Lorilleux and his cowardice in their presence: 'en
face d'eux, elle le voyait bien, il faisait le chien couchant...
était aux cent coups quand il les croyait fâchés. Et cela, simplement, inquiétait la jeune femme pour l'avenir' (p. 108). When
Mme Lorilleux on their wedding-day rudely exclaims: 'Tu vas
coucher dans la chambre à la Banban!', Coupeau responds
only to the insulting nickname, but Gervaise takes the full
measure of her meaning: 'elle entendait bien... la chambre à la
Banban, c'était la chambre où elle avait vécu un mois avec Lantier, où les loques de sa vie passée traînaient encore' (p. 120).
She is also immediately sensitive to the changed attitude of
the Boche couple in the presence of M. Marescot (p. 160),

and when an eviction is mentioned, she wonders percipiently
whether such a thing could ever happen to her, if she should
fall on hard times. Gervaise also wins our admiration by her
courage in innumerable small acts, like the way she deals with
the Lorilleux when they torment her, after Coupeau's accident, about the shop she had set her heart on renting. To show
that her sacrifice is made with a good heart, she accompanies
each withdrawal from her savings with a brave joke at her own
expense: 'Je sors, je vais louer ma boutique' (p. 149).

Gervaise's patience, courage and sensitivity win our sympathy and assent, as does her constant, and only too well-
grounded fear of the world, vividly evident from the first
chapter. Her confused apprehensiveness is dramatized in specific responses like the dread that grips her on moving into
the giant building of the rue de la Goutte-d'Or (p. 158), and
which, in her youthful optimism, she dismisses. Her sense of her
own weakness reinforces her fear of bad company, expressed
in terms that send us back to the title of the novel and ultimately acquire the force of a prediction: 'la mauvaise société,
disait-elle, c'était *comme un coup d'assommoir,* ça vous cas-
sait le crâne, ça vous aplatissait une femme en moins de rien'
(p. 68, my italics). Zola underlines, throughout the narrative,
the looming shadows that perpetually threaten Gervaise's life
and happiness, using the verbal equivalent of film back-
ground-music to alert the nerves and arouse apprehension.
Menace builds up from the framing of Gervaise's life between
the hospital and the abattoir, from the vision of Paris swallow-
ing the herds of workers, from the gaping jaws of the apartment
building, and, on Gervaise's wedding-day, the flashes of light-
ning, in which Gervaise seems to see 'des choses graves, très
loin, dans l'avenir' (p. 97). The old woman who watches
Coupeau working on the roof, as if waiting for him to fall
(pp. 143-46), the thirteen at the *fête,* and the sinister song of
Bru, all operate like musical passages to create an atmosphere
of threat. The smooth whirring of the production-belt in the
roof of Goujet's foundry sounds like the wings of a night bird,
and this is later echoed in the sound of Bazouge's cape,
brushing against the wall 'avec le bruit d'ailes d'un oiseau de
nuit' (p. 388), and we feel the haunting presence of death.

Alongside the menace of the surrounding world, runs the menace within Gervaise herself. Having accustomed us to Gervaise's basic honesty and good sense, Zola makes us all the more sensitive to the progress of Gervaise's weaknesses and the degeneration of her indulgent devotion to Coupeau into indiscriminate tolerance and self-indulgence. She, who earlier worked with such energy and nursed Coupeau with such self-less generosity, begins to resent the demands of her work – 'à la fin c'était son tour de jouir un peu' (p. 241). Her weariness and discouragement are understandable but none the less indicative of a grave deterioration of character, which is conveyed in a multitude of tiny details.

Zola uses physical sensation, gesture and movement to reflect a subtle and intuitive understanding of the psychology of his characters, and this is particularly evident in the treatment of the relationship between Gervaise and Goujet. The Goujet family stands in striking contrast to the 'mauvaise société' of the *faubourgs,* and Goujet is the successful outcome of the nurture v. nature, or environment v. heredity battle, waged against the threatening legacy of a drunken and criminally violent father. Gervaise's relations with Goujet offer tantalizing glimpses of what might have been, and provide insights into her emotions. Goujet's shyness is obvious from the start – after accidentally surprising her half-dressed, he cannot look her in the eye for a week. He watches her admiringly while she nurses Coupeau, and he sits quietly gazing at her as she works in the laundry. Gervaise basks in his undemanding affection, learning to rely on him more and more – 'Quand il lui arrivait quelque ennui sérieux, elle songeait au forgeron; ça la consolait' (p. 188). As the family situation worsens, the need for consolation increases and Goujet becomes a haven of decency and the foundry a refuge. Gervaise's first visit to the foundry arises from confused sensations in which external atmosphere, languor and a vague yearning for gratification all combine:

> Il avait plu le matin, le temps était très doux, une odeur s'exhalait du pavé gras; et la blanchisseuse ... étouffait un peu ... remontant la rue avec la vague préoccupation d'un désir sensuel, grandi dans sa lassitude. Elle aurait volontiers mangé

quelque chose de bon ... elle aperçut la plaque de la rue Marca-
det, elle eut tout d'un coup l'idée d'aller voir Goujet à sa forge.
(p. 198)

Physical sensations convey Gervaise's unrecognized emotional need as she turns to Goujet for a comfort she cannot find
elsewhere and this confusion of moral and physical needs will
play a large part in Gervaise's downfall, as she grows ever more
apt to substitute physical satisfactions for the moral ones that
elude her.

In the foundry, Goujet and Bec-Salé improvise a competi-
tion, each taking his own huge lump of metal to hammer into
shape. Gervaise realizes that the display of prowess is for her
benefit, and Zola transcribes her thoughts in the mode of free
indirect speech, with brief but telling interpolations of his own
greater linguistic resources, to create a partly colloquial and
partly poetic articulation of her feelings: 'Mon Dieu! que les
hommes étaient donc bêtes! Est-ce que ces deux-là ne tapaient
pas sur leurs boulons pour lui faire la cour! ... Faut-il avoir
des inventions, n'est-ce pas?' (p. 207). From this familiar
'spoken' effect, the language moves up a notch, while still
retaining much of the rhythm and character of the spoken
word: 'Le cœur a tout de même, parfois, des façons drôles de
se déclarer. Oui, c'était pour elle, ce tonnerre de Dédèle et de
Fifine sur l'enclume; c'était pour elle, tout ce fer écrasé; c'était
pour elle, cette forge en branle, flambante d'un incendie, em-
plie d'un pétillement d'étincelles vives. Ils lui forgeaient là un
amour...' (p. 207).

Here Zola has stepped in to translate Gervaise's pride in
this heroic scene, but he keeps close to Gervaise's own voice,
adopting here, as so often elsewhere, the tone and language of
the *quartier*: 'Et, vrai, cela lui faisait plaisir au fond; car enfin
les femmes aiment les compliments'. Now the language again
moves up the scale: 'Les coups de marteau de la Gueule-d'Or
surtout lui répondaient dans le cœur; ils y sonnaient, comme
sur l'enclume, une musique claire qui accompagnait les gros
battements de son sang'. This brief heightening is immediately
followed by a return to a style in which the use of the deictic
'ça' and 'là' and the indefinite 'quelque chose' combines with

hesitation and repetition to suggest the intimacy of Gervaise's feelings: 'Ça semble une bêtise, mais elle sentait que ça lui enfonçait quelque chose là, quelque chose de solide, un peu du fer du boulon... maintenant, elle se trouvait satisfaite, comme si les coups de marteau de la Gueule-d'Or l'avaient nourrie' (pp. 207-08). The rhythmic hammer-strokes provide a sublimated consummation of the love of Goujet and Gervaise.[16]

The idyllic relationship with Goujet provides a temporary haven, but this too is lost when Gervaise is driven by Coupeau's filth into the arms of Lantier. At first she feels guilty and disgusted with herself for having succumbed, but the habit of indulgence and complaisance now extends to herself, generating a resigned and helpless acceptance for the sake of peace – 'pourvu que son mari et son amant fussent contents, que la maison marchât son petit train-train régulier, qu'on rigolât du matin au soir, tous gras, tous satisfaits de la vie et se la coulant douce, il n'y avait vraiment pas de quoi se plaindre' ... 'son dévergondage avait tourné à l'habitude' (p. 329). Goujet's discovery of her relations with Lantier marks a further point in her progressive loss of self-respect and hope. She returns from the encounter with Goujet and his mother 'de l'air bête des vaches qui rentrent chez elles, sans s'inquiéter du chemin' (p. 336), already on the path toward dehumanization that her life henceforth will follow. The death of Maman Coupeau sets the seal on the degeneration of Gervaise's life and marks the beginning of the end.

The stages of Gervaise's decline, and her awareness of it, are filtered through the words, gestures and silences of many incidents. Particularly telling is the way Zola intertwines the change in the relations of Gervaise and Goujet with the events of Maman Coupeau's funeral. We learn almost parenthetically, in the midst of the family squabbles and funeral arrangements, that the money Lantier is taking to pay the undertaker includes 'soixante francs que Gervaise était allée emprunter à Goujet, en cheveux, pareille à une folle' (p. 355). The swift

---

[16] This scene, with its marked rhythms and its connections with 'Le Forgeron' (*3*, pp. 454-58), is interestingly discussed in *22*, pp. 254-57.

explanation offers a glimpse of a desperate Gervaise, out of control, turning almost automatically to Goujet to help her out. The reader, by this stage, can make the same tacit assumption of Goujet's unfailing generosity, but the very elision of the borrowing-scene underlines Gervaise's unthinking use of Goujet and creates a sense of unease.

As Gervaise joins the funeral procession, she meets up with Goujet. From 'la blanchisseuse' and 'Goujet', the narrative moves into the greater intimacy of 'il' and 'elle'. He joins the men, but greets her so tenderly 'qu'elle fut reprise par les larmes. Elle ne pleurait plus seulement maman Coupeau, elle pleurait quelque chose d'abominable, qu'elle n'aurait pas pu dire, et qui l'étouffait' (p. 365). In the 'quelque chose' we are made to feel Gervaise's shameful recognition of her reckless folly, her betrayal of Goujet, and her loss of her own better self. After the ceremony, when Coupeau offers drinks to the company, Gervaise lags behind to try to persuade Goujet to join them, but he says he must get back to work – 'Alors, ils se regardèrent un moment, sans rien dire' (p. 367). The silence is eloquent.

Gervaise tries to make amends, but her words unwittingly emphasize her abuse of Goujet's devotion: 'Je vous demande pardon pour les soixante francs, murmura enfin la blanchisseuse. J'étais comme une folle, j'ai songé à vous...' (p. 367). Goujet interrupts these lame words to tell her it is all right and she is forgiven, but asks her not to tell his mother 'parce qu'elle a ses idées, et que je ne veux pas la contrarier' (p. 367). Goujet's response too is heavily charged with unstated meaning in its oblique acknowledgement of a contravention of the rules of honesty and decency – even demoted, as they are here, to the status of Mme Goujet's 'notions'. At this point, we move again from 'la blanchisseuse' and 'le forgeron' to the more intimate personal pronouns, as Gervaise fluctuates again between remorse and the temptation to exploit:

> Elle le regardait toujours; et, en le voyant si bon, si triste, avec sa belle barbe jaune, elle fut sur le point d'accepter son ancienne proposition, de s'en aller avec lui, pour être heureux ensemble quelque part. Puis il lui vint une autre mauvaise

pensée, celle de lui emprunter ses deux termes, à n'importe
quel prix. Elle tremblait, elle reprit d'une voix caressante:
"Nous ne sommes pas fâchés, n'est-ce pas?" (p. 367)

This scene with Goujet demonstrates particularly well the
subtlety and psychological skill that Zola is sometimes said to
lack. The alternations of tense, between imperfect and past
historic, show Gervaise's movements as she is drawn from ap-
praising Goujet to the impulse to take him up on his earlier
offer, then to another 'mauvaise pensée'. That it is she who
recognizes it as 'mauvaise' is indicated by the fact that it leaves
her trembling, but she still begins to act on it ('elle reprit'),
using a 'voix caressante' for her first move.

Goujet's reply is simple but final for both of her ideas: 'Lui,
hocha la tête, en répondant: "Non, bien sûr, jamais nous ne
serons fâchés... Seulement, vous comprenez, tout est fini." '
Goujet then strides away, but his reply reverberates in her
head as she enters the wineshop, her shock turning into a sort
of sullen rage and self-pity: 'elle entendait sourdement au fond
d'elle: "Tout est fini, eh bien! tout est fini; je n'ai plus rien à
faire, moi, si tout est fini" ' (p. 368). With the feeling that this
is the end of her, she turns to filling her mouth with food and
draining a glass of wine. With simple phrases and physical
gestures, with no explicit psychological analysis, Zola indicates the far-reaching impact of Goujet's words and the sullen
self-disgust that fills Gervaise. Will, energy and self-respect
have drained away into impotence and moral inertia; only the
bodily comforts remain. When Lantier and Coupeau then join
forces to make Gervaise give up her shop, she goes on eating
ravenously, and gives up on the shop too, with another echo
of Goujet's words: 'Je m'en fiche pas mal de la boutique! Je
n'en veux plus... Comprenez-vous, je m'en fiche! Tout est
fini!' (p. 369).

The mistake of Bazouge, who thinks it is Gervaise who is
to be buried, is all the more disturbing in that he is not far
wrong, that a good deal of Gervaise is indeed to be buried with
Maman Coupeau, as Gervaise herself realizes: 'ça devait être
un morceau de sa vie à elle, et sa boutique, et son orgueil de
patronne, et d'autres sentiments encore, qu'elle avait enterrés

ce jour-là' (p. 370). The elliptic 'd'autres sentiments encore' sounds the death-knell for the Gervaise Goujet loved.

The move upwards in the building, to the new tiny apartment, 'dans le coin des pouilleux', marks a further descent and brings another moment of cruel self-awareness for Gervaise. Remembering herself as she was long ago, looking up hopefully into the building, she now reflects that 'elle n'était plus en bas... la figure vers le ciel, contente et courageuse' (p. 372). She is high up now, almost too fat to get into the window-embrasure to look out, and her face is turned earthwards, towards death. Her longing for sleep, for peace, becomes a longing for death and a terrified fascination with Bazouge. Coupeau's entry into the hospital, on the roof of which he had earlier worked, provokes further reflections on the profound change in their life, again expressed in simple spatial terms: 'il n'était plus sur les toits, pareil à un moineau rigoleur et putassier; il était dessous... Mon Dieu, que le temps des amours semblait loin, aujourd'hui!' (p. 400). It is the 'Assommoir' itself that gives the *coup de grâce,* and as she accepts the first glass of liqueur (an anisette that recalls her childhood drinking), Gervaise's mind goes back to the day when she ate the brandied plum with Coupeau – 'En ce temps-là, elle laissait la sauce des fruits à l'eau-de-vie. Et maintenant, voici qu'elle se remettait aux liqueurs. Oh! elle se connaissait, elle n'avait pas pour deux liards de volonté' (p. 409). This recognition does not save her; indeed, it has already an edge of excusal and abdication of responsibility.

Once she has embarked on her last self-destructive phase, Gervaise's humanity begins rapidly to fade, and indeed she ceases for a while to dominate the perspective of the narrative. Nana takes her place in more than one sense for the whole of the eleventh chapter. The breaking of the heart and spirit of Gervaise is re-enacted in the crushing under Coupeau's heel of Nana's beloved heart-shaped locket (p. 431), and just as Gervaise seemed to be pushed by the full force of the neighbourhood into the arms of Lantier, so Nana is pushed toward sexual corruption by the over-insistent prohibitions of Coupeau and the ever-present temptations of the milieu. Other parallels between the mother and daughter reinforce the sense

of inexorable processes. The warmth and smell of the road
after rain, that seemed to feed the languor of Gervaise before
her visit to Goujet's foundry, are echoed in the similar stimulus
given to Nana's greedier desires – 'elle sentait monter du pavé
de Paris une chaleur le long de ses cuisses, un appétit féroce de
mordre aux jouissances' (p. 434), and just as Gervaise was
driven from the filth of Coupeau to the cleaner sheets of
Lantier, so Nana is driven to escape from the comfortless slum
her home has become – 'le papa pochard, la maman pocharde,
un tonnerre de Dieu de cambuse où il n'y avait pas de pain
et qui empoisonnait la liqueur. Enfin, une sainte ne serait pas
restée là-dedans' (p. 435).

When Nana leaves home, Zola offers brief moments of
access to Gervaise's thoughts, which show how far she has
sunk from the woman she once was. Having helped by her
mode of life to drive Nana into prostitution, she sinks into
self-pity, blaming Nana and seeing her flight as a final humiliation – 'Oui, ce chameau dénaturé lui emportait le dernier
morceau de son honnêteté dans ses jupons sales' (p. 436) – and
she has now become too brutalized even to feel the shame of
it for long. During the long descent into sloth and depravity,
there are, however, intermittent reminders of Gervaise's natural
generosity of spirit. It is she who cries 'Mais on ne peut pas la
laisser massacrer!' (p. 233) and goes to the rescue of Mme
Bijard – followed by Bru, with whom she is more and more
intimately associated in the later stages of the novel. After the
death of Mme Bijard, Gervaise befriends Lalie, who serves as
both positive and negative counterpart to Gervaise. The child-
mother, with her womanly patience and endurance recognizes
in Gervaise a friend and ally, but also comes to see in her the
terrible face of her brutal father – 'ce souffle d'eau-de-vie, ces
yeux pâles, cette bouche convulsée' (p. 413). The mute accusa-
tion of Lalie's 'regard noir' which follows Gervaise as she
staggers by is one of many landmarks in Gervaise's terrible
descent: Lalie's death, as we shall see, is another.

Zola makes us feel directly the brutalization of Gervaise,
reflecting the coarsening of her consciousness in the coarsening of her language and responses. When Coupeau is taken off
to Lariboisière with pneumonia, Gervaise bitterly recalls the

time when she would have fought to keep him at home, but
'ces beaux sentiments-là n'ont qu'un temps, lorsque les
hommes tombent dans la crapule' (p. 399). Even then, when
the stretcher-bearers come, she cannot bear to see him carried
away 'comme un meuble', and wishes she had the money to
keep him. By the time of Nana's departure, there is a marked
deterioration. Gervaise goes for weeks without thinking of her
daughter, and when she does, her reaction ranges randomly
between love, violent anger and a sense of outraged owner-
ship – 'Elle finissait par n'avoir plus une idée bien nette de
l'honnêteté. Seulement, Nana était à elle, n'est-ce pas? Eh
bien! lorsqu'on a une propriété, on ne veut pas la voir s'évapo-
rer' (p. 447). This muddying of her consciousness – and con-
science –increases steadily as she falls ever lower into an animal
existence of drunkenness, wretchedness, hunger and violent
fights with Coupeau. Disgust with him and the world in general progressively blots out other reactions, till her attitude is
summed up in the coarse obscenity of impotent rage: 'Oui,
dans le derrière, son cochon d'homme! dans le derrière, les
Lorilleux, les Boche et les Poisson! dans le derrière, le quartier
qui la méprisait! Tout Paris y entrait, et elle l'y enfonçait d'une
tape, avec un geste de suprême indifférence, heureuse et
vengée pourtant de le fourrer là' (p. 464).

When the Lorilleux refuse any help when she is starving,
she shows no emotion: even anger and self-pity have given
way to mute exhaustion and despair – 'Gervaise traîna ses
savates dans le corridor, alourdie, pliant les épaules' (p. 470).
Zola now allows little access to her inner world, presenting
her far more from the outside, making the reader feel there is
little lucid consciousness left in her, and he makes us aware
of her numbness in the face of events as we follow her dragging
footsteps. The groans of the dying Lalie Bijard temporarily
rouse her from her torpor, and she goes in to the child, and
snatches the whip away from Bijard when he returns maddened
by drink. The sight of Lalie's battered and scarred body over-
whelms her with pity, but unable to do anything, Gervaise
leaves, filled once more with impotence and disgust at life – 'la
vie était trop abominable! Ah! quelle sale chose! ah! quelle sale

chose! Et Gervaise partit ... sans savoir, la tête perdue...'
(p. 474).

With the image of Lalie imprinted on her mind, Gervaise,
tormented by hunger, sets out on her long, solitary walk, and
her last, long 'monologue', after which she will sink out of
reach into an animal existence and finally, death. [17] Her body
walks as it wills, and goes searching for Coupeau, but he has
nothing to offer save sardonic encouragement to go and find
a man. Gervaise finds herself once more alone and abandoned
(like the 'Enfant du Bon Dieu' of Mme Lerat's song), lost in
the crowd of workers returning home, until she looks up to
see before her the Hotel Boncœur, where, twenty years ago,
she had lived with Lantier, and where, of course, the novel
began. The wheel has come full circle. The morning crowd at
the opening has given way to the evening crowd at the close –
'Ah! oui, Gervaise avait fini sa journée!' (p. 482) – and Gervaise takes measure of the terrible distance she has come.

As she walks through the cold and the dark, Zola surrounds
her with images from the 'journée' of her life. She sees the
'Assommoir' lit up like a cathedral for a High Mass (p. 485),
and as she clumsily solicits the passing men with 'Monsieur,
écoutez donc', she passes the Lariboisière hospital and the
abattoirs – 'C'était sa promenade dernière, des cours sang-
lantes où l'on assommait, aux salles blafardes où la mort
raidissait les gens dans les draps de tout le monde. Sa vie avait
tenu là' (p. 487). At this moment of painful recognition of her
life's boundaries, she is shocked into further self-awareness by
the sight of her shadow on the ground beside her – 'Mon Dieu!
qu'elle était drôle et effrayante! Jamais elle n'avait si bien
compris son avachissement' (p. 488). Snow begins to fall, and
Gervaise continues her quest. At last a man stops, but, as she
approaches, he holds out a begging hand. Gervaise the street-
walker recognizes Bru the beggar: 'A cette heure, ils pouvaient
se donner la main' (p. 490).

---

[17] Jacques Dubois admirably comments: 'le long soliloque de Gervaise au
chapitre XII sera comme un ultime sursaut, la protestation d'un *je* qui rend
les armes' (*23*, p. 84).

The final and terrible irony of Gervaise's 'promenade dernière' comes when she approaches a possible customer, who turns out to be Goujet. In the lamplight, Gervaise, who once was 'aimée... pareillement à une sainte vierge' (p. 188) by this man, sees again her hideous rollicking shadow dancing beside her. As Goujet gazes at her, the snow seems to scatter white daisies in his golden beard – as if to recall the dandelions he scattered in Gervaise's basket as they sat long ago on the waste ground near Montmartre. This meeting with Goujet makes Gervaise ask: 'qu'avait-elle donc fait au bon Dieu, pour être ainsi torturée jusqu'à la fin?' (p. 491), underlining the contrast with the 'Enfant du Bon Dieu' who, when abandoned by the human world, receives, unlike Gervaise, the protection of God.

Few words are exchanged in the encounter, but a great deal is said through action, gesture and description. Gervaise waits humbly outside until Goujet, speaking in a low voice as if his now dead mother might still hear, tells her to come in. Closing the door of his room behind them, he tries, seized by a sudden rage, to crush her in his arms. Gervaise's 'Oh! mon Dieu! ... oh! mon Dieu!...' (p. 492) makes Goujet realize her terrible hunger, and he gives her food, which she gulps down ravenously, stammering her thanks, bursting into tears at the first mouthful. Goujet sees the snow melting on her grey hair, her pitiful, fat and ugly old body, and recalls their youthful love, his long-frustrated desire. Gervaise, having eaten, sits with lowered head, not knowing what Goujet now wants or expects. When she undoes a button of her blouse, Goujet falls to his knees and stops her – 'Je vous aime, madame Gervaise, oh! je vous aime encore et malgré tout, je vous le jure!' (p. 494).

Overcome by pain and shame, Gervaise begs him to get up. In what amounts almost to a parodic version of the earlier scene when Goujet proposed an elopement, Goujet respectfully requests the favour of a kiss, while Gervaise reflects: 'Mon Dieu! elle était à lui, il pouvait faire d'elle ce qu'il lui plairait' (p. 494). The emotional impact of this scene owes a great deal to Zola's sensitive notation of gestures and movements, and also to the patterning of events – a patterning by which the memories of the characters are supplemented by the reader's textual memories, giving events the depth and resonance they have in the framework of a life's experience. Subjacent to the vision of Gervaise gulping down Goujet's food – with Goujet giving her water to prevent her from choking – lie other previous incidents: Gervaise going to the foundry with a vague longing, as for something nice to eat, and coming away satisfied; her gormandizing at her *fête,* 'seulement un peu honteuse devant Goujet' (p. 259); and her compulsive eating in her despair after Goujet's 'tout est fini'. Here, it is starvation that subjugates Gervaise to her animal needs – and her tears are no doubt as much tears of relief as tears of shame.

Zola does not need to spell out the cruel ironies that under-pin the scene; they are evoked in gestures and actions, snatches of memory in Goujet, and a few very simple, half-choked words. From Gervaise, the narrative offers no memories at all; she is completely absorbed by eating and sobbing. The only access we are given to her consciousness is when she wonders what Goujet expects of her, picked up as she has been, like any street-walker; again, when she cries out at Goujet's kneel-ing declaration of love – 'j'ai trop de honte ... pour l'amour de Dieu! relevez-vous. C'est ma place, d'être par terre' (p. 494); and finally her nodded 'Yes' when, overcome with emotion at his respect, she indicates that he may kiss her, aware that she can be had for the price of a meal. Goujet simply kisses her forehead, then falls on his bed, sobbing. And Gervaise can do nothing but try to express her recognition that the situation is unendurable, and go away: 'Je vous aime, monsieur Goujet, je vous aime bien aussi ... Oh! ce n'est pas possible, je com-prends ... Adieu, adieu, car ça nous étoufferait tous les deux' (p. 494).

She goes away in a sort of mental blank, like the stupor that seized her on leaving the dying Lalie, and returns to awareness only when back at the rue de la Goutte-d'Or. There, images of death crowd around her; she enters the darkness of the building as if going into 'une gueule ouverte' (p. 495); the courtyard looks like a cemetery and the dyer's stream runs black over the snow. As she mounts the long stairs, she is shaken by terrible laughter as she recalls her ideal of long ago, and all the illusions and delusions long since shattered. Of her

dream of retiring to the country after twenty years of work, all
that remains is the longing for her 'coin de verdure au Père-
Lachaise' (p. 496). It is only after a survey of her life and
broken dreams that Goujet resurfaces in her almost demented
mind – 'Au fond, sa grosse douleur venait d'avoir dit un adieu
éternel au forgeron' (p. 496). The last thread that joined her
to her former, better self is broken, and miseries crowd in upon
her. She sees Lalie, now dead, through the open door as she
goes by, and envying her peace, Gervaise goes to Bazouge and
begs him to carry her away to sleep for ever. The drunken
Bazouge jokes at her wild pleas, and Gervaise is left regret-
ting that 'la misère ne tuait pas assez vite' (p. 498). But she is
already virtually dead. Only a phantom figure remains, and
in the final – and thirteenth – chapter, Zola makes us feel
acutely the numb emptiness that now inhabits her body, making her a lifeless puppet that merely twitches a while until
death at last comes to her relief.

She has become indifferent to Coupeau's frequent disap-
perances, and the notification she receives from the hospital
means to her only that 'son cochon était en train de crever à
Sainte-Anne' (p. 499). Fury that Coupeau had been on a long
drinking bout with Mes-Bottes without ever offering her a
drink, cuts off any other reaction. The following day, however,
the letter begins to bother her and she sets out on the long
walk to see him. The sight of Coupeau whirling about in his
padded cell fills her with terror and she is glad to escape from
his ravings into the fresh air outside. Back at the apartment
block, everyone is agog to hear details of Coupeau's strange
affliction and Gervaise does a horrifying imitation of Coupeau's dance. If her mind refuses reflection, her body has
taken the impact and reproduced it.

The next day Gervaise decides not to go back, but a brutish
curiosity – 'Ça serait curieux pourtant, s'il faisait toujours ses
ronds de jambe' (p. 504) – drives her to return. Coupeau is still
dancing and screaming. The doctor, asking about the inci-
dence of alcoholism in Coupeau's family, turns on Gervaise
herself, to ask 'Vous buvez aussi, vous?' (p. 506) and despite
Gervaise's lying protestations, insists: 'Vous buvez! Prenez
garde, voyez où mène la boisson ... Un jour ou l'autre, vous

mourrez ainsi' (p. 506). Gervaise now seems little more than an indifferent spectator at Coupeau's death-agony, and her inadequate observation needs the extra perspective afforded by the watching doctors. Back in the rue de la Goutte-d'Or, the neighbours are agog for the latest news of the freak, and eager to see her repeat her Coupeau imitation. Fear now makes her refuse, but when they stop asking, she unwittingly falls into the imitation. As the company applauds, 'elle resta hébétée, ayant l'air de sortir d'un rêve' (p. 510). Zola's shift of the perspective here views her from the outside, as one 'seeming' to emerge from a dream, emphasizing the growing lack of consciousness in Gervaise and the narrative distance this imposes. She is no longer there to be plugged into; and it is through the eyes of the Boches that we see Gervaise setting out again the next day.

At Sainte-Anne, she is again an insensitive, inadequate spectator. She has a brief moment of terror when Coupeau speaks to her in his delirium, and she recognizes Coupeau's re-enactment of his trade, but no reaction is recorded. When Coupeau talks of 'le chapelier', the doctor asks Gervaise to explain, and his bafflement points up the remoteness of the doctors from the life-story the reader knows so well, and at the same time shows Coupeau and Gervaise now as objects of observation rather than the surrogate observers they once were. Coupeau is incomprehensible in his madness, and Gervaise can only stammer inarticulately. They are both locked in a story that has become, for them, literally unspeakable. When Coupeau falls to the floor, Gervaise joins the doctors around the prostrate, but still shaking body, and her reaction to the terrible tremors of his flesh is a crude mixture of curiosity, fascination and impersonal horror – 'Quel sacré travail! un travail de taupe! C'était le vitriol de l'Assommoir qui donnait là-bas des coups de pioche' (p. 515). When at last Coupeau's feet stiffen and he is dead, no response is recorded from Gervaise. The narrative moves brusquely from 'La mort seule avait arrêté ses pieds' to 'Quand Gervaise rentra rue de la Goutte-d'Or...' (p. 515).

On her return, Gervaise makes her announcement brutally: 'Il est claqué, dit-elle en poussant la porte, tranquillement, la

mine éreintée et abêtie. Mais on ne l'écoutait pas' (p. 515).
The death-agony, whose progress had been followed like a
circus performance, has ceased to command attention. Coupeau's death is stripped (as Gervaise's will be) of all dignity
and significance in the *quartier*. The scandal of the Poisson
household, where Virginie has been caught *in flagrante delictu*
with Lantier, is now the topic of conversation. Coupeau's
sisters dutifully bring out their handkerchieves when the news
at last penetrates, but Boche dismisses the subject with 'Bah!
c'est un soûlard de moins!' (p. 516).

Like Coupeau's feet which danced on long after their owner was dead in all save the clinical sense, the body of Gervaise
goes on, and the narrative perspective becomes even further
distanced, with months of her life curtly summarized – 'Gervaise dura ainsi pendant des mois' (p. 516). Only her body
remains alive, with its intermittent miming of Coupeau's
death-dance. She dies alone and unnoticed like an animal in
the 'trou' where Bru preceded her. Only the drunken Bazouge
is left to show her some last brief tenderness as he gathers her
up: 'Va, t'es heureuse. Fais dodo, ma belle!' (p. 518).[18] That
last moment is resonant with memories – of Gervaise's long
yearning for rest and sleep, her fear of the drunken *croque-
mort* outside the hotel Boncœur on her wedding-night, her
horror at Bazouge's coming for her when called for Maman
Coupeau, her terrors at living in the room next to his, her
increasing fascination with him, her crazed pleas to him to
end her misery and carry her away. At last, the haunting
prediction of Bru's 'Trou-la-la' is fulfilled, along with the
'Laissez-moi dormir' of Gervaise's song. The 'Fais dodo, ma
belle!' of Bazouge hits all the harder because Gervaise is virtually excluded from this last chapter of her history. It is her
absence that we follow, in a remorselessly indifferent world,
through the last pages of the novel. But Zola finally returns
her to the centre of the stage, to recall, with tragic irony,

----

[18] Bazouge is prefigured in Zola's story 'Mon voisin Jacques', where Jacques, the *croque-mort,* promises the narrator 'de me porter en terre, lorsque le
moment serait venu, avec une douceur de main tout amicale' (*3,* 435-39,
p. 438).

through the drunken tenderness of the *croque-mort,* the reality
and the dreams of the decaying object Gervaise has become.

Gervaise is ample testimony to Zola's ability to create
convincing and vivid characters. We may feel Lalie Bijard to
be over-saintly, Goujet a shade too heroic, and the Lorilleux
too irredeemably monstrous, but they too are vividly drawn,
and they serve as polarizations of the moral vision. Goujet
may be 'dur d'intelligence', but he is 'bon tout de même'
(p. 136). He is the would-be educator of Coupeau, having the
will and energy to resist hereditary and environmental pressures
and to work with dignity and pride; he has the resolution to
offer Gervaise a way out from the crushing prison of her life
with Coupeau, and even to detach himself, despite his abiding
love, when Gervaise returns to Lantier. Lalie is a dramatic
expression of Zola's sense of outrage at the victimization and
destruction, by the combined forces of ignorance, alcohol and
poverty, of innocence and goodness. She epitomizes in miniature, and in simpler form, the scandals we are made to feel
more broadly throughout the novel, much as Coupeau's hallucinations condense the vicissitudes of his life. Zola uses strong
colours, but as Auerbach remarks, 'if Zola exaggerated, he did
so in the direction which mattered' (*10,* p. 512).

I have concentrated thus far on the human 'figures in the
web', and among them, on the central figure of Gervaise. But
there is another sense of 'figure' which is also relevant here –
'figure' as part of the movements of a dance. In outlining the
centrality of Gervaise, we have seen the interweaving movements of the other dancers of *L'Assommoir,* as each one joins
a ring of victims or persecutors. The dances revolve around a
wider primary figure – the circle formed by the cavernous mouth
of Paris – and within that, the yawning gullet of the building
in the rue de la Goutte-d'Or. Gervaise, at first a frightened
bystander, is drawn into the centre of a ring, where she enjoys
an early success, radiating contentment into a world of which
she appears to have taken possession: 'La rue de la Goutte-
d'Or lui appartenait, et les rues voisines, et le quartier tout
entier' (p. 167). She smiles at the world, and it smiles back.
Around her, other dancers circle, changing their positions, but
always interlinked, and intermittently entering her ring or

pulling her into theirs. She moves away from and then towards
Bazouge and death; she protects and then replaces Bru; her
idyllic 'pastorale' with Goujet turns into a hideous shadow-
dance; she changes partners from Lantier to Coupeau, then
partners both and then neither; she moves into shifting
alliances and hostilities with the Boches, with Virginie, and the
whole *quartier.*

As the mood darkens, the dance grows violent, and then
macabre, until at the end, the circle of dancers breaks up,
leaving behind the lifeless body of Gervaise in the arms of
death. It is like the ending of a tragic ballet, and, as in a ballet,
the choreography of Gervaise Macquart's life is rich in symbolic suggestion. That symbolic choreography, imposed by the
elaborate patterning of the narrative, is the subject of the next
chapter.

3

The Closed Horizon

L'ASSOMMOIR is elaborately structured, with alternations of private and public life, and changes of scene which reflect changes of mood and condition and suggest contrasts, parallels and echoes from one scene to another. The women's fight in the wash-house, for instance, is echoed in the duel between Goujet and Bec-Salé; the wedding of Gervaise and Coupeau is part of a series of major family events – Nana's birth, baptism and first communion, Maman Coupeau's death and funeral. Gervaise's happy perambulations around the rue de la Goutte-d'Or in the days of her triumph find a dour echo in her desperate walk through the streets in the penultimate chapter. The break-up with Lantier is followed by the successive courtships of Coupeau and Goujet, and the persistent siege of the returned Lantier. The dancing in the music-halls is hideously parodied in Coupeau's *danse macabre*. The forge of the Lorilleux contrasts with the forge of Goujet's foundry, and both connect associatively with the stoves of the *lavoir* and of Gervaise's laundry. Gervaise's ideal of a happy life recurs throughout the novel as aspiration, fulfilment, and finally, bitter memory.

The changing situations combine with changes of value, as things swing between positive and negative poles to create, ultimately, a tragic vision of closure, entrapment and dehumanization. Gervaise's first view of the Lorilleux forge is negative; she is repelled by the dirt and the heat, but she will come to view the same scene as an inaccessible haven of warmth and food. Goujet's forge is a mixture of the diabolic and the godlike. The rue de la Goutte-d'Or is the focus of both fear and desire, while Gervaise's laundry, her pretty sky-blue shop, dedicated to cleanliness, becomes a nest of dirt and decay. Into the midst of this artfully organized structure of places and events are worked more intricate themes. Before moving on to consider the subtler thematic strands that Zola weaves in and through the diverse episodes of the novel, it will be helpful to examine the interplay of some of the larger structuring shapes in the interconnections between the Lorilleux forge, the forge of Goujet, and Gervaise's laundry.

In her first encounter with the Lorilleux forge, Gervaise finds the couple in 'une pièce étranglée, une sorte de boyau' (p. 76), working at their gold, Lorilleux's knotty fingers moving 'avec une vivacité de singe' (p. 77). Their almost mechanical absorption in their work and the coldness of their welcome make an indelible impression. Later in the novel, they are described as living 'une vie d'araignées maigres' (p. 385). The repeated animal imagery adds a dramatic edge, and at the same time underlines the brutalization of humanity in this atmosphere of poverty and corruption. The Lorilleux are small, thin and twisted, like their gold, and utterly mean-spirited. In answer to a complaint in 1877 about the vileness of the characters of *L'Assommoir,* Zola acknowledged the nastiness of the Lorilleux, but pointed out that they are 'les esclaves et les victimes de la petite fabrication en chambre ... La même besogne abrutissante les cloue pendant des années dans un coin étouffant, sous le feu de leur forge qui les dessèche'.[19] They work desperately hard, and whatever youth they ever had is gone – as is made clear through Gervaise's eyes (p. 77). Gervaise is cruelly disappointed at finding her future in-laws so unfriendly, their rooms so mean and ugly, and the gold only strands of what looks like black wire.

A second visit to the Lorilleux forge is placed just before Gervaise's first visit to Goujet's foundry to strengthen the associative pattern of forge, foundry and laundry. Gervaise's first view of the foundry, in the light of a spurt of flame from the furnace, is so deeply patterned by her own experience that the foundry seems converted into a gigantic and grotesque laundry: 'Des toiles d'araignée pendaient aux poutres, comme des haillons qui séchaient là-haut, alourdies par des années de

[19] Letter to the editor of *Le Bien public* in 1877, in *21,* p. 56.

saleté amassée' (p. 200). Later, Gervaise's laundry, in its decay, is described in terms that recall this scene: 'l'humidité des linges séchant au plafond avait décollé le papier; la perse pompadour étalait des lambeaux qui pendaient pareils à des toiles d'araignée lourdes de poussière' (p. 337). The negative view of the foundry, loaded with the dirt of years, is reinforced by the shrivelled animal figure of Bec-Salé, with 'sa barbe de bouc et ses yeux de loup' (p. 205) and *eau-de-vie* in his blood-stream. In striking contrast with the negative aspect, the golden figure of Goujet with his strength, his untainted blood and his neck white as a child's, strikes the heroic note. In a reversal of the disappointment caused by the Lorilleux gold – 'ce métal noirâtre, vilain comme du fer' (p. 78) – the base metal, iron, acquires under Goujet's hammer the dignity and grandeur of the precious metals: 'L'enclume avait une sonnerie argentine' (p. 202), and Goujet's hair and beard form a golden halo round his head, while memories of the sculptures seen in the Louvre seem to colour Gervaise's vision (p. 207). The idealized view of Goujet in this scene, although primarily a reflection of Gervaise's feelings, also owes a good deal to Zola's view of the nobility of human toil. In a sketch entitled 'Le Forgeron' (1874), which reads like a blue-print for the figure of Goujet, Zola presents the smith as a modern answer to the heroes of classical antiquity – 'Il m'apparaissait comme le héros grandi du travail, l'enfant infatigable de ce siècle... qui façonne dans le feu et par le fer la société de demain...' (*3*, pp. 454-58).

The juxtaposition of the Lorilleux forge and Goujet's foundry not only brings out the distinctive emotional colorations of the characters, but helps to impose a fundamental polarity that animates and structures the novel – the aspiration to a humanity creative, heroic and god-like and the horror of a humanity animalized and mechanized. Goujet, 'une vraie figure d'or', seen as 'beau, tout-puissant, comme un bon Dieu' (pp. 206, 207), becomes a figure of apotheosis, while the Lorilleux, 'd'une dureté abêtie de vieux outils, dans leur besogne étroite de machine' (p. 194), are exemplars of reification.

Despite the simplicity of most of the language, the scene in the foundry takes on the colours of a heroic joust, in which the desiccated, demonic figure of Bec-Salé is contrasted with the controlled and graceful strength of Goujet. After his victory, Goujet takes Gervaise's hand 'comme s'il l'avait conquise' (p. 208), and shows her the new machinery which is being installed. Here Zola combines realist observation with the impact on Gervaise of this strange and frightening place, to create a quasi-supernatural effect. Gervaise becomes aware of what sounds like whirring wings, and her gaze is drawn upwards 'au vol souple des courroies, dont elle regardait... la force énorme et muette passer dans la nuit vague des charpentes' (p. 210). That sense of animate power heightens Goujet's fears that the new machines will replace human effort with their mechanical strength: 'Un jour, bien sûr, la machine tuerait l'ouvrier' (p. 211). His fears are, however, mitigated by the thought that 'peut-être que plus tard ça servira au bonheur de tous' (p. 211). Perhaps indeed, machines will ultimately liberate rather than enslave Man's creative energy, but in the meantime, after seeing the uniform products of the machines, Gervaise reassures Goujet: 'J'aime mieux les vôtres. On sent la main d'un artiste, au moins' (p. 211), acknowledging a creative power not shared by the machines – nor by the mechanized Lorilleux.[20] Madame Goujet makes a similar recognition of individual 'art' when she acknowledges the personal stamp of Gervaise's work: 'Allez, je reconnais votre main tout de suite' (p. 213).

The fierce heat of the Lorilleux apartment and the foundry is echoed by the heat of the laundry – its stove constantly over-fed by Augustine. But the heat of the laundry, originally associated with hard work, and also seen positively as a refuge for the cold and the hungry, becomes a negative element, linked with Gervaise's growing laziness. The heat and the smell of the dirty washing combine to create a stale and corrupting atmosphere that seems to affect first Gervaise's physical movements and then her very soul: 'il semblait que ses *premières*

---

[20] Robert Lethbridge (*31*, pp. 133-34) draws attention to Zola's contrasting of the mechanical labour of Lorilleux (as a 'possibly ironic mirror' of 'the Zola who had planned *La Chaîne des êtres*') and the art of the 'forgeron créateur' (as a Vulcan reflecting the novelist's creative and shaping force).

paresses vinssent de là, de l'asphyxie des vieux linges empoisonnant l'air autour d'elle' (p. 174, my italics). The use of 'premières' here, as in the reference to Coupeau's drunken embrace as 'une *première* chute dans le lent avachissement de leur vie' (p. 178) firmly prophesies the decline.

The *fête* which seems the high point of the life of the laundry in fact marks its virtual end. With Lantier's entry into the family, and Coupeau's rapid degeneration, the accumulated filth of the milieu – its dirty linen and its moral corruption – takes over Gervaise's shop and her life. Dirt itself becomes a kind of warmth in which her growing indifference is cradled: 'Même la saleté était un nid chaud où elle jouissait de s'accroupir... sentir la maison s'alourdir autour de soi dans un engourdissement de fainéantise, cela était une vraie volupté dont elle se grisait' (p. 338). The same themes return again and again, warmth, abandon and intoxication. Zola makes the steamy heat of the laundry a symbol of torpor and sloth. And just as the laundry, at first an instrument of cleanliness, gradually succumbs to the encroaching dirt, the very concepts of cleanliness and dirt – both physical and moral – grow confused in Gervaise's mind, so that when she finally accepts prostitution, she reflects: 'Sans doute, ce n'était guère propre; mais le propre et le pas propre se brouillaient dans sa caboche, à cette heure; quand on crève de faim, on ne cause pas tant philosophie...' (p. 479).

In the penultimate chapter of the novel, a destitute Gervaise, tortured by hunger and cold, tries to beg or borrow from the Lorilleux. As the door opens, she inwardly exclaims: 'Comme il faisait bon, là-dedans!' (p. 466), and almost faints with hunger at the smell of the soup. The tantalizing presence of gold is all around her, and although the room is dirty and ugly as ever, 'elle le voyait resplendissant de richesses' (p. 468). The change of vision – in the opposite direction from that of Gervaise's laundry – sharply underlines the moral and material defeat of Gervaise and the triumph of the Lorilleux. Deaf to Gervaise's pleas, they refuse to help and are left exulting, 'joliment vengés des anciennes manières de la Banban, de la boutique bleue, des gueuletons, et du reste' (p. 469). The carefully orchestrated parallels and contrasts between the two forges and the laundry (and the associated characters), strengthen the structure of the novel and dramatize the conflicts between, on the one hand, the creative energy of the human will and spirit, and, on the other, the animalizing and mechanizing powers of the sloth, alcoholism and greed fostered by deprivation and ignorance.

The broader pattern represented by the whole claustrophic world of the Paris *faubourgs* embodies Zola's sense of the profound frustration of the lives of the poor. It is this frustration, he argues, in the article addressed to the ruling classes in 1872 (quoted in the Introduction), that makes the working-class man turn to drink – 'parce que vous lui fermez l'horizon, et qu'il a besoin d'un rêve'. An intricate pattern of references and images sets the closed world of the *faubourgs* against the haunting backdrop of a shadow world of aspiration and dreams denied.

As Flaubert's Emma Bovary dreams of Paris on the basis of its name printed on her pot of pomade, Zola's Parisians dream of the country on the strength of a blade of grass, a patch of blue sky, a glimpse of the Seine or even a snatch of song, like the one Clémence sings at Gervaise's *fête* – 'ça rappelait la campagne, les oiseaux légers, les danses sous la feuillée, les fleurs au calice de miel' (p. 270). Hiding from the rain under the Pont-Royal on Gervaise's wedding-day, the ladies sit pulling up grass from between the paving-stones, 'regardant couler l'eau noire, comme si elles se trouvaient à la campagne' (p. 104), and Mlle Remanjou remembers a youthful love beside the banks of the Marne (p. 104). In the rue Neuve-de-la-Goutte-d'Or, a single acacia lends delight to the whole street for Gervaise, and makes Coupeau remember a country visit of his childhood (p. 127). During the early years of their marriage, Gervaise works out that if they go on working and saving for twenty years, they will be able at last to retire to the country (p. 138);[21] meanwhile, they make week-end visits to Vincennes or Saint-Ouen with the Goujets. The

---

[21] Joy Newton (*31*, 67-73) admirably analyses Zola's presentation of the countryside as a persistent element of Gervaise's ideal and comments that 'as her horizons shrink, so do her dreams' (p. 67).

countryside is always present as an ideal, beckoning amidst the Parisian grime. Indeed when Coupeau gets out of Paris and goes to work in Etampes for three months, it proves its real healing powers when he stops drinking, and comes back 'frais comme une rose' (p. 373). The idea of the country, for the inhabitants of the *faubourgs,* seems the very emblem of escape; it is the privileged setting for the poetry of life, for dreams of love and happiness.

When Goujet takes Gervaise's hand in the darkness of the foundry, their brief intimacy is as sweet as if they were 'seuls dans le bois de Vincennes ... au fond d'un trou d'herbe' (p. 208). Nostalgia for the country haunts Zola's city, underlining all that it is not, suggesting the notion of a natural paradise in contrast with the urban hell. In the enfolding heat of the laundry in winter, when snow lies thick on the ground, muffling the street-noise, Gervaise feels as if she were in the country (p. 218), and as she makes her way to the refuge of Goujet's forge, she is filled with a gaiety that converts the waste-land, the grey factories, the road black with coal-dust, and the puffing chimneys, into 'un sentier de mousse dans un bois de la banlieue, s'enfonçant entre de grands bouquets de verdure' (p. 230).

Gervaise's meeting with Goujet on the patch of ground between a sawmill and a button-factory, where a tethered goat bleats on the parched grass and a dead tree crumbles in the sun, similarly becomes a pastoral idyll – 'Vrai! murmura Gervaise, on se croirait à la campagne' (p. 302). Such vivid responses effectively highlight the longings that wring delight from such piteous landscapes. The two sit together looking at the rows and rows of grey and yellow houses, the distant patches of sparse greenery, 'et quand ils renversaient la tête davantage, ils apercevaient le large ciel d'une pureté ardente sur la ville, traversé au nord par un vol de petits nuages blancs. Mais la vive lumière les éblouissait'. Dazzled by the light, they turn their gaze back to the distant blur of the *faubourgs* on the flat horizon, while beside them, a pipe from the sawmill rhythmically puffs out its steam, and 'Ces gros soupirs semblaient soulager leur poitrine oppressée' (p. 302). There is nothing in this scene to offend the demands of realism, but there is a powerful symbolic undertow in this translation into physical reality of the inarticulate feelings that can only be expressed by a mechanical steam-pipe, and the blocked dreams and darkness of lives now incapable of facing too much light.

When Gervaise has reassured Goujet that she has not gone back to Lantier, they sit silent, Goujet holding her hand.

> Au ciel, le vol des nuages blancs nageait avec une lenteur de cygne. Dans le coin du champ, la chèvre, tournée vers eux, les regardait en poussant à de longs intervalles réguliers un bêlement très doux. Et, sans se lâcher les doigts, les yeux noyés d'attendrissement, ils se perdaient au loin, sur la pente de Montmartre blafard, au milieu de la haute futaie des cheminées d'usine rayant l'horizon, dans cette banlieue plâtreuse et désolée, où les bosquets verts des cabarets borgnes les touchaient jusqu'aux larmes. (p. 304)

The swan-clouds, the gentle bleating of the goat, the clumps of greenery, create, in the 'banlieue plâtreuse et désolée', a pastoral scene that seems the very image of their dreams at once so close and so far away. Here Goujet suggests running away together to Belgium and Gervaise turns the offer down, as if again dazzled by a too bright light. Goujet finds comfort only in clambering about on his knees, gathering dandelions, and Gervaise leaves with a basket full of bright flowers as if, indeed, after a day in the country.

In the midst of reminders of how Gervaise's life is bounded 'entre un abattoir et un hôpital' (p. 51), of how sunlight and sky are blocked by buildings – 'des maisons de quatre étages barraient le ciel' (p. 126) – Gervaise's shop, decorated in blue and yellow with floral wall-paper, creates a private haven: '...elle trouvait sa boutique jolie, couleur du ciel. Dedans, on entrait encore dans du bleu; le papier ... représentait une treille où couraient des liserons' (p. 163). It is as if she were trying to recapture the blue sky and sunshine of Plassans – which she recalls with nostalgia in the wash-house in the early pages of the novel: 'Ça sentait meilleur qu'ici... Il fallait voir, il y avait un coin sous les arbres ... avec de l'eau claire qui courait...' (p. 34). When Coupeau first talks to Gervaise of the apartment block in the rue de la Goutte-d'Or – 'On serait bien ici, n'est-ce

pas?', Gervaise agrees: 'Oui, on serait bien, murmura Gervaise', but adds: 'A Plassans, ce n'était pas si peuplé, dans notre
rue...' (p. 67). When 'cette belle boutique bleue, couleur du
ciel' (p. 337) falls into decay, the destruction of Gervaise's
dream of that far-off country is made physically visible.

At the end of the novel, the physical horizon, ironically,
opens out as a result of the demolitions: 'Maintenant, de la
rue de la Goutte-d'Or, on voyait une immense éclaircie, un
coup de soleil et d'air libre' (p. 447). But this comes too late
for Gervaise. Her personal horizons are closed – 'le quartier
s'embellissait à l'heure où elle-même tournait à la ruine. On
n'aime pas, quand on est dans la crotte, recevoir un rayon en
plein sur la tête' (p. 448). In Gervaise's last walk, the contrast
between the light, space and handsome buildings of the new,
and the ruins and tatters of the old *quartier* again stresses the
fact that if new horizons are opening in Paris, they are not
opening for the likes of Gervaise. Against the 'horizon lumi-
neux de Paris' Gervaise makes out the corner of the blackened
roof of the railway station, and standing on the railway bridge,
she takes her last look at the lost countryside of her dreams.
A train sets out from Paris and all she sees is its steam, but
she feels the vibration of the bridge; 'elle-même restait dans le
branle de ce départ à toute vapeur' (p. 484). The physical
vibration of the bridge (suggestively recalling the 'branle' of
Goujet's forge) is also the vibration of Gervaise's longings, and
she turns as if to follow the invisible train hurtling towards a
desired but unseen landscape – 'De ce côté elle devinait la
campagne, le ciel libre ... Oh! si elle avait pu partir ainsi, s'en
aller là-bas, en dehors de ces maisons de misère et de souf-
france! Peut-être aurait-elle recommencé à vivre' (p. 484).
Then with a movement touching in its naturalness at this
moment of defeat and despair, she turns to the notices stuck
on the bridge, and stands there 'lisant stupidement'. One of
the notices is, mockingly, a pretty shade of blue, and it offers
a reward of fifty francs for a lost dog. 'Voilà une bête qui avait
dû être aimée!' is the cry which rises from Gervaise's heart.

That contrast between the loved animal and the starving
Gervaise, nerving herself for prostitution, marks the end of all
hope. After the terrible last encounter with Goujet, she is

racked by bitter laughter as she recalls her old ideal – 'travailler tranquille, manger toujours du pain, avoir un trou un peu propre pour dormir, bien élever ses enfants, ne pas être battue, mourir dans son lit' (p. 495) and her old dream of retiring to the country (p. 496). The only 'countryside' left to hope for now is her bit of greenery in the cemetery of Père Lachaise.

The notion of 'la campagne', which returns so insistently to haunt the urban landscape, obviously represents more than a frustrated fondness for greenery and fresh air. The countryside has the force of a haunting metaphor for a mythic elsewhere – a lost innocence, a *paradis perdu*, like a memory of the childhood of the world from which the novel's city-dwellers are forever excluded. Zola inscribes that metaphor into the texture of daily life in the *faubourgs,* colouring the contemporary urban scene with the deep sense of loss that animates his vision. A few snatched moments of happiness seem to be all that can be hoped for in a city where a benevolent nature has no place, and where a herded humanity, deprived of air and light, is increasingly brutalized and mechanized.

The haunting absence of 'la campagne' is matched by an insistent absence of 'le bon Dieu'. The religious rituals that punctuate life from birth to death seem mere concessions to tribal convention, with no spiritual dimension. The mass for the Coupeau marriage is haggled over with 'un vieux petit prêtre, en soutane sale, voleur comme une fruitière' (p. 87). Coupeau grudges the money but 'un mariage sans messe, on avait beau dire, ce n'était pas un mariage' (p. 87). The mass is dispatched by a priest whose haste and indifference are described in terms that comically suggest the jerky agitation of a clockwork toy: 'mangeant les phrases latines, se tournant, se baissant, élargissant les bras, en hâte, avec des regards obliques sur les mariés et sur les témoins' (p. 91). The members of the wedding-party remain outsiders, intruders in an unfamiliar, alien world. The bride and groom are in confusion about when to stand, sit and kneel, while the witnesses opt for standing all the time to avoid mistakes, and Maman Coupeau weeps into a borrowed missal. The marriage ceremony takes place to the accompaniment of hammering from the main altar where new hangings are being attached, and the sound and dust of the beadle sweeping up. A scowling priest, briskly running his gnarled hands over the heads of the couple, 'semblait les unir au milieu d'un déménagement, pendant une absence du bon Dieu' (p. 91). The 'bargain' religious ceremony is totally overshadowed by the social occasion, and 'le bon Dieu' will remain conspicuously absent.

Nana's christening is also a social rather than religious ritual 'Coupeau ne voyait guère la nécessité de baptiser la petite; ça ne lui donnerait pas dix mille livres de rente, bien sûr; et encore ça risquait de l'enrhumer. Moins on avait affaire aux curés, mieux ça valait' (p. 132). Maman Coupeau, however, scolds him for being a 'pagan', and the Lorilleux clearly regard the baptism as an indispensable sign of respectability. The ceremony itself is passed over in silence, in favour of the dinner that follows, and the christening presents.

The next major 'ceremonial' event is the death of Maman Coupeau, which takes place on a night when Gervaise is sleeping with Lantier. Gervaise looks for Maman Coupeau's crucifix, until she remembers it has been sold. When Maman Coupeau's daughters arrive, Mme Lorilleux insists on having a lighted candle beside the body, and Mme Lerat borrows a crucifix from a neighbour, a wooden cross so big it seems to crush Maman Coupeau's body. Then Nana is sent to the church for a bottle of holy water, and at last the scene is arranged according to custom, but with no hint of spiritual significance. The burial is the next question, and Lantier brings information on the undertakers' prices (p. 353). The funeral arrangements, interspersed with the noisy singing of Nana and the children laughing and playing out in the yard, become a cause of dispute, with Mme Lorilleux predictably resolved to spend as little money as possible – 'On ne ferait pas revenir maman, n'est-ce pas?' (p. 353). Gervaise, however, insists on a mass and a nice hearse, so that Maman Coupeau will be respected in death and not cast into the earth 'comme un chien'.

The visiting neighbours all make the sign of the cross and piously scatter holy water. M. Marescot is the only visitor who thinks of praying, but as soon as he has completed his devotions, he informs the Coupeaus that if they fail to pay their overdue rent, they will be evicted in two days (p. 357). The gap between outward ritual gesture and inner feeling could hardly be clearer. While Gervaise shows a genuine respect for the human if not the divine, Marescot's hypocrisy shows respect for neither God nor Man. The religious ceremony takes place with a dispatch that recalls the Coupeaus' wedding, though the mass is slower 'parce que le prêtre était très vieux' (p. 366). M. Madinier is made the spokesman for a brutal denunciation of the priests and their doings: 'ces farceurs-là, en crachant leur latin, ne savaient seulement pas ce qu'ils dégoisaient ... sans avoir dans le coeur le moindre sentiment ... Et tous les hommes lui donnaient raison' (p. 366).

Nana's first communion is interspersed with family squabbles and concerns that have little to do with the religious aspect of the ceremony. Quickly surveying her fellow-communicant, Pauline Boche, Nana is relieved to find her 'moins bien mise qu'elle, arrangée comme un paquet' (p. 380), while Mme Lorilleux makes the most of having provided Nana's dress and indulges her characteristic malice. Coupeau, however, affected by a hymn, dissolves into tears. His reaction – a mixture of the maudlin sentimentality of the drunkard, and some genuine stirring of emotions and memories – soon gives way to resentment and self-justification once he returns to the familiar world of the bar: 'il accusa les corbeaux de brûler chez eux des herbes du diable pour amollir les hommes ... ses yeux avaient fondu, ça prouvait simplement qu'il n'avait pas un pavé dans la poitrine. Et il commanda une autre tournée' (p. 381). Whatever momentary spiritual influence the Church and its music may have exerted is soon drowned in drink and the exclusively secular gaiety of the Poissons' house-warming that follows in the evening. For Nana and Pauline, the first communion serves as an induction into womanhood rather than a spiritual initiation: 'On leur parla même de leur mariage et des enfants qui leur pousseraient un jour. Les gamines écoutaient et rigolaient en dessous' (p. 383). In the course of the evening, Nana's future career as a florist is decided, and Mme Lorilleux's malicious comment:

'Encore une roulure pour les boulevards' (p. 383) will prove prophetic.

In the penultimate chapter of the novel, Mme Lerat's song 'L'Enfant du bon Dieu', returns to mind when Gervaise prays to God to hold off the threatening snow. But 'le bon Dieu' is shown here as an inoperative concept whose invocation signals delusion. There is no transcendent Court of Appeal in Gervaise's life, and she wonders what she has done to be thus tormented, with a sense of injustice that recalls Coupeau's bitter comment after his fall: 'S'il y a un bon Dieu, il arrange drôlement les choses' (p. 152). The 'lost paradise' of the country is matched by the loss of hope of any spiritual Paradise. The real 'Church' of the Coupeaus and their associates is the 'chapelle' of gluttony into which the shop is transformed on Gervaise's saint's-day, the pawn-shop to which Maman Coupeau eagerly scuttles with 'la mine confite et gourmande d'une dévote qui va à la messe' (p. 339), and the 'cathédrale' of the 'Assommoir', where 'on célébrait la Sainte-Touche, quoi! une sainte bien aimable, qui doit tenir la caisse au paradis' (p. 485). Drink is what provides the comfort of the poor, the gateway out of their closed, bleak world into an artificial paradise. Despite their awareness of the Church's calendar, and their observance of the basic religious rites, 'le bon Dieu' figures more in blasphemy than in prayer, and money-grubbing priests treat the poor with indifference or contempt.

A third strand in Zola's tapestry shows the world of art and culture hovering mockingly around them, threaded through their lives as if to underline their fundamental exclusion from it, and the tragic waste of human vitality and creative energy. The zest and aptitude Gervaise shows in the arrangement and decoration of her shop are matched by the skill of her ironing. Coupeau, early on, is not only a likeable fellow with his cheeky Parisian wit and his comic songs, but also a skilled craftsman, whom we see, just before his disastrous fall, singing on the rooftop, while, 'penché sur son établi, il coupait son zinc en artiste' (p. 144). The wedding-guests show great pride in their various crafts (p. 111) and Poisson, the one-time cabinet-maker, works with apparently inexhaustible patience at the little ornamental boxes which are his passion (p. 216). Goujet is elevated to a heroic level on which he wields his hammer with an artist's hand, and he adorns his virginal room with pictures cut out of illustrated papers;[22] Gervaise tries to re-create the colours and flowers of the country in her shop. There is a touching description of the rooms in the rue Neuve-de-la-Goutte-d'Or, where the young couple have reached out into the cultural deposits of the world about them to adorn their new home with a jumble of discordant bric-à-brac (p. 126). But art and literature belong, like the countryside, in a world apart. The sense of distance, of exclusion from the cultural world, is kept alive throughout the novel by Zola's use of sustained cultural counterpoint. The ignorance, lack of taste, vulgarity and sometimes gross insensitivity of the members of this level of society are not allowed to conceal their humble but genuine aspirations, nor the frustration of their dreams.

Zola uses the visit to the Louvre to etch in the relationship between his characters and the world of art. The scene is rich in comedy, but it is a comedy tinged with the pathos of clumsy attempts to bridge the gap between their world and the world of culture. Music too is intricately woven into the fabric of the novel in metaphors and persistent references, ranging from the popular songs of the *fête* to the music of the dance-halls, the 'sacrée musique de désespoir' of the apartment-block and the *danse macabre* which ends Coupeau's life.

It is above all the sense of the closed horizon that animates these patterns of repetition. They embody Zola's deep sense of outrage at the abasement of a humanity born to dignity and grandeur. The repeated animal imagery (the wolf-like Bec-Salé, Coupeau the 'cochon', Gervaise who dies of 'avachisse-ment', Mme Le*rat,* the 'troupeau' of workers) reinforces this theme, while other images suggest the reification of humanity (Nana, the spinning top, the puppet Coupeau, the Lorilleux

---

[22] Philippe Hamon recalls the similar habit of cutting out pictures in other Rougon-Macquart characters, seeing this as a reflexive allusion to the work of the novelist himself who, 'lui aussi, crée souvent des personnages d'après des "coupures" de journaux (par exemple les Bijard, dans *L'Assommoir*)' (*27,* pp. 50-51).

with their 'dureté abêtie de vieux outils'). Against this reductive picture of human life, Zola sets the tenderness of Gervaise, the heroic 'figure d'or' of Goujet, the energy and hopefulness of the young Gervaise and Coupeau, the aspirations, dreams and nostalgias of the workers, their pride in their work and skills.

The demented visions of Coupeau, as he dances to death, allow Zola a freedom unavailable to a realist writer within the frame of normality. John Hemmings, discussing the insanity and the lunatic asylum in *La Conquête de Plassans,* comments: 'The madhouse breaches the closed circle of naturalism, and through the gap we glimpse distant vistas of an eternal pattern working itself out beyond nature and rational comprehension. By the accent he puts on apparently gratuitous details, the artist draws attention to this opening...' (*28,* p. 105). In Coupeau's hallucinations, Zola is able to describe a series of visions that form a condensed and symbolic version of Coupeau's life, just as, earlier, a dream condenses the pattern of Gervaise's life: 'elle rêva qu'elle était au bord d'un puits; Coupeau la poussait d'un coup de poing, tandis que Lantier lui chatouillait les reins pour la faire sauter plus vite. Eh bien! ça ressemblait à sa vie' (p. 343).

Starting significantly with an Edenic vision of greenery and singing waters, Coupeau moves through the classic horrors of *delirium tremens,* as through a macabre parody of the torments and vicissitudes of his life. He is pricked by pins, and tormented by a grotesquely phallic snake-like creature, cold and slimy, that lies upon his thighs and bites. Everything he drinks, from soup to lemonade, turns instantly into *eau-de-vie.* The walls move and Coupeau screams at imagined priests who ring bells and play the organ to drown his cries for help (a symbolic reflection of his, and Zola's, sense of the Church as an irrelevant obfuscation). He hears the rumble of a machine behind the walls then fire breaks out and flames create a vision of Hell (pp. 506-08).

In a second set of visions (pp. 510-13), Coupeau fights with what seems an army of bugs, then he mimes his old craft, using his bellows, soldering the zinc, but enemies are all around him, sending troops of rats against him, and spiders that crawl all over him. Then, in a dramatic enactment of the mechanization of Man, his own belly seems to become a steam engine (the very emblem of the new industrial society), and from his mouth he puffs out dense smoke, which fills the cell, goes out through the window, and rises in the sky, blotting out the sun. From the window he seems to watch a cavalcade that recalls the images of animalization spread through the novel, and Clémence appears with her hair full of feathers as if representing both her own promiscuity and that of Nana whose feathered hat identified her to Gervaise and Coupeau as it bobbed about in the throng of the dance-hall. Soldiers appear with their guns trained on him, as if to recall the *coup d'état* and the régime imposed by force of arms. Then the houses crumble, and Coupeau imitates the noises of 'un quartier qui s'écroule' – recalling the great demolitions. Next he seems enmeshed in Gervaise's hair, and as he pushes her away, he sees 'le chapelier' hiding behind her skirts, and falls upon him, fists flying, with savage threats and oaths, until defeated, he falls into 'une lâcheté d'enfant'. Screaming for help, he watches while Lantier cuts off Gervaise's legs and carves her in two, then he backs away with screams of terror, and collapses on the floor, seeming dead – apart from his feet which still dance on.

This emblematic 'morality play' which begins in a childhood Eden of innocence and ends in Hell, gains further impact when set alongside a much earlier 'apparently gratuitous detail', introduced into Gervaise's boutique on the day of her public embrace by the drunken Coupeau – an incident quite heavily underlined as 'une première chute dans le lent avachissement de leur vie' (p. 178). The detail in question is merely an unexpected adornment on the ironing-table: 'Un bouquet de grands lis, dans un ancien bocal de cerises à l'eau-de-vie, s'épanouissait, mettait là un coin de jardin royal, avec la touffe de ses larges fleurs de neige' (p. 179). The royal lilies make their appearance in the midst of a description of the women bent silently over their tasks. Coupeau, quiet at this point, soon becomes troublesome again, and makes gross advances to Clémence until he is pushed away by Gervaise into the bedroom. Gervaise accepts, tolerates and indulgently

pardons his behaviour, and the laundry returns to the peaceful
activity of the women as they ply their irons in the overpowering heat. Zola describes the smells of the laundry in which
overheated metal, stale starch and the sweating women all
intermingle, before he returns once more to the lilies: 'le
bouquet de grands lis, dans l'eau verdie de son bocal, se fanait,
en exhalant un parfum très pur, très fort' (p. 185).

The detail of the lilies in the laundry is sufficiently conspi-
cuous by its placing and repetition to justify attention. One
reason for this 'apparently gratuitous detail' is of course the
contrast it marks between the white purity of the lilies (in an
old *eau de vie* bottle now holding water) and the steamy
corruption, both physical and moral, of the laundry. But the
lilies are not only white but majestic – creating around themselves, in the midst of the irons and the washing-baskets, 'un
coin de jardin royal', and adding the touch of royalty to the
long series of 'countryside' images. At the end of the episode
of the 'première chute', the water has turned green, and the
lilies have wilted. The symbolism is clear: the royal garden of
innocence withers after the Fall, leaving behind only the scent
of its purity. The evanescent royal garden seems an emblem
of that Eden at the heart of the pattern of references to the
country, the 'paradis perdu' of the city-dwellers. Here, at the
moment of the moral Fall of the Coupeau family, physically
prefigured by Coupeau's fall from the roof, the Eden of innocence is briefly glimpsed in the fading lilies whose scent
lingers in the air, like the nostalgia that haunts the minds of
men.

The myth of pre-lapsarian Man, lord of creation in his
pristine innocence, is pervasive in Zola's work, and it will be
useful here briefly to consider its wider context. Already in
one of Zola's early stories, 'Le Sang', a soldier dreams of a
world of whiteness, where Man's innocence 'le sacrait roi des
autres êtres de la création' (*3*, p. 56), until Cain's spilling of
the blood of Abel stains the world with the redness of guilt.
This myth of royalty, a central element in Zola's mythopoeic
vision, and an avatar of the Romantic myth of the 'no-
ble savage', permeates the fabric of the Rougon-Macquart

novels.[23] In the last of the cycle, *Le Docteur Pascal,* Charles
Rougon (great-grandson of tante Dide and Rougon, the original,
legitimate couple), afflicted with the 'royal' disease of haemo-
philia, bleeds to death, his blood ebbing away over pictures of
the kings and queens of France. The royalty myth makes its
most explicit appearance in *La Faute de l'abbé Mouret* (1875),
in which Zola presents his own secular version of the Christian
myth of the Fall,[24] set in a garden significantly named 'Le
Paradou'. Here, before their Fall, the two lovers 'marchaient
royalement dans la foule des animaux qui leur rendaient obéis-
sance' (*2,* I, 1391, my emphasis).

The 'coin de jardin royal' which makes its transitory appearance in Gervaise's laundry seems an echo of this pervasive
myth and gives a tragic resonance to the degradation writ large
in the pages of *L'Assommoir.* But even without stepping outside the context of *L'Assommoir* itself, the 'royal garden' of the
lilies heightens and intensifies the nostalgia for Man's lost
paradise which animates the long succession of allusions to
Nature and 'la campagne'. The theme recurs in the penultimate
chapter, when Gervaise, starving and in despair, recalls her
youth and a far-off day when she was chosen to be 'queen' of
the laundry (p. 483). Gentlemen stopped to stare as she passed
'comme pour une vraie reine'. In a passage that recalls Baudelaire's image of the sick negress wretchedly wandering the
Paris streets,

> Piétinant dans la boue, et cherchant, l'œil hagard
> Les cocotiers absents de la superbe Afrique
> Derrière la muraille immense du brouillard[25]

Zola takes us into Gervaise's inner monologue, then shifts the
viewpoint almost imperceptibly to show her from the outside:

---

[23] See Michel Butor's stimulating essay on this subject in *18.*

[24] I have discussed elsewhere the symbolic significance of this novel – in
'Zola's mythology: that forbidden tree', *Forum for Modern Language Studies,*
XIV, 3 (July, 1978), pp. 217-30.

[25] Baudelaire, *Les Fleurs du mal,* Paris, Garnier, 1961, p. 96.

> Reine, oui, reine! avec une couronne et une écharpe, pendant vingt-quatre heures, deux fois le tour du cadran! Et, alourdie, dans les tortures de sa faim, elle regardait par terre, comme si elle eût cherché le ruisseau où elle avait laissé choir sa majesté tombée. (p. 483)

The evocation of Gervaise's lost majesty[26] is immediately followed by the sight of the abattoirs and the stench of blood from their 'façade éventrée', and then the hospital with its 'porte des morts' (p. 483).

Without moving implausibly outside the narrative constraints imposed by his largely inarticulate characters, Zola threads the novel with images, metaphors and references that create intricate and insistent thematic patterns and transform the material of his documentation and observation into the fibres of a work of art. The realist texture of Zola's presentation of an everyday and often squalid reality is interwoven with glimpses of a more heroic and mythic world, beyond the closed horizon, a world in which humanity would have the dignity and majesty to which, in Zola's view, it was born. Zola's aesthetic explicitly demands an impersonal and neutral view of an accurately observed reality, but the controlled tension between the realist foreground and the mythic patterns against which it is set provides powerful expression of a personal and passionate vision.

[26] David Baguley (*12*, p. 117) comments on the studied placement and effect of this 'lost majesty' passage, which 'curiously unrelated to any previous event in the novel, functions like the *mise en abyme,* as a microcosmic, generic reading of the heroine's fate, but also ... serves to promote the heroine to a higher literary status'.

Conclusion: 'The coarse, comprehensive, prodigious Zola'

CRITICAL assessments of the writer whom Henry James called 'the coarse, comprehensive, prodigious Zola' (*29*, p. 473) have not only differed but differed extremely, some seeing him as poet and visionary, some as a myopic 'greffier' with no creative genius, and others as a crude and dated popular novelist lacking in artistry. The last few decades have seen a widespread reappraisal of Zola's artistic status and integrity, and a general recognition of his artistry and the powerful imaginative and mythic structures that underpin his work. It is natural, in such reappraisals, for critics to seek out those elements in the writer's work that relate him to contemporary literary modes and issues. In Zola's case this is not difficult. His concern for social justice and human dignity remains all too relevant to our own era, and like other great writers who withstand the test of time, Zola is both profoundly of his own time and of ours. Naomi Schor, for instance, is able, without risk of absurdity, to claim Zola as 'an ingenious and instinctive structuralist' (*36*, p. 35).

Zola's concept of the novel as 'experimental' chimes to a certain extent with the stress on 'le roman comme recherche' that characterized the *nouveau roman* of the 1960s, and his highly conscious preoccupation with language also gives him a modernist aspect. That aspect is reinforced by his sophisticated narrative strategies, his use of a wide range of 'cinematic' techniques (panorama and close-up, fades, flash-backs, etc.), and his studied manipulation of 'point-of-view': even the self-conscious reflexivity and the use of *mise-en-abyme* associated with the *nouveau roman* may be discerned in Zola's

pages. [27] Philippe Hamon, in a recent major study, emphasized
the functionalism of Zola's characters and stressed the modern-
ism of what he sees as a tendency to fragmentation and a
relative lack of individuation in Zola's characterization, which
he associates with similar tendencies in the *nouveau roman* of
the 1960s (*27*, p. 322). I would argue, however, that Zola does
not reject individual characterization, and that his treatment
of characters is very far removed from the largely faceless and
often nameless inhabitants of the *nouveau roman*. While the
characters are open to multiple and very diverse interpretations
– when viewed through lenses as diverse as Marxist, sociological, structuralist, epistemological, formalist, feminist, nar-
ratological, or linguistic – Zola does not deliberately cultivate
ambiguity in his characters, nor does he renounce authorial
omniscience as the *nouveaux romanciers* do.

Zola's characterization has long been – perhaps inevitably,
given the monumental scale of his work and his choice of
subject – an area of particular contention. Henry James, who
placed Zola among 'the men of largest responding imagination
before the human scene' (*29*, p. 473), remained somewhat
scandalized by the lack of cultivated individuals and psychological complexity in Zola's novels, and the consequent reduc-
tion, as it seemed to him, of the nature of man, in *L'Assommoir*, to the mere play of instincts (*29*, p. 410). [28] 'His "psychology", in a psychologic age, remains comparatively coarse',
James observed. But this, he went on to say, only draws attention to 'the miracle', by which the intrinsically 'common' is
transformed and 'taught to receive into its loins the stuff of the
epic' (*29*, p. 415). While rightly stressing Zola's epic qualities,
James does less than justice to Zola's 'psychology', even while
acknowledging that his characters have 'almost insupportably,

[27] Most obviously in *Nana* and *Le Docteur Pascal,* but also, more discreet-
ly, elsewhere (see, for instance notes 20, 22 and 26 above).

[28] A rather similar view to James's presides over the chapter on *L'Assommoir* by Ian Gregor and Brian Nicholas in *The Moral and the Story,* London,
Faber & Faber, 1962 (pp. 63-97). They denounce the 'purely surface representation' (p. 108) which results, in their view, from the constraints of Zola's
'objective' aesthetic and the moral inadequacy of his characters.

the sense of life' (*29*, p. 418). So strong a 'sense of life' demands and demonstrates psychological insight of a very high order, though very different from the refined intricacies we find in James's characters. The reader of *L'Assommoir* is drawn into a bond of common humanity with Gervaise, in her progressive abdication of responsibility and 'honnêteté', her capitulation to facile self-justification and self-pity, and the agonized moments of recognition that punctuate the process of decay. The physical and the concrete become, in Zola's hands, rich vehicles for the moral and psychological.

Zola's capture, on the page, of the very muscle and pulse of his characters involves the reader deeply in each moment of their lives, and each moment carries a mythic charge from a network of interwoven patterns. Zola does not present the highly complex and introverted beings found in the psychological novel, and minor members of his huge casts necessarily remain somewhat rudimentary, but the central characters of Zola's novels are nevertheless sharply individuated in their flesh, bone and blood as well as in their temperaments, temptations and aspirations. Zola seems to enter, by imaginative empathy, into his characters and their situations, adopting their perspective and their terms, as they encounter a world based on the closely observed realities of late nineteenth-century France. But that world is assimilated into a vision that transcends the historical frame.

Zola's realist-naturalist endeavour and his poetic-mythopoeic impulse are not in conflict. They work wonderfully well together. We might well ask, along with Michael Wood, 'What if realism were not averse to allegory and symbolism but habitually incorporated them? What if myth in literature were not a method but a horizon and climate, a region where the imagination, whatever its ambitions, could not but end up?'[29] Zola provides weighty support for that hypothesis: the objects and gestures he perceives, the features of everyday life he observes and studies are no less real for being absorbed

---

[29] Wood, Michael, Review of Margaret Lowe, *Towards the Real Flaubert: a study of 'Madame Bovary'*, *French Studies* XLII, 2 (April 1988), p. 220.

into a moral and aesthetic vision in which, for Zola, as for Baudelaire,

> ...palais neufs, échafaudages, blocs,
> Vieux faubourgs, tout pour moi devient allégorie.[30]

[30] Baudelaire, *Les Fleurs du mal,* Paris, Garnier, 1961, p. 96.

Selective Bibliography

W ORKS are referred to in this study by their italicized number in this list.

ZOLA'S WORKS

All references to the text of the novel (and the accompanying *Dossier*) are to the Folio edition (*1* below).

1. *L'Assommoir,* edited and annotated by Henri Mitterand, with a preface by Jean-Louis Bory, Paris, Gallimard, 1978.
2. *Les Rougon-Macquart,* sous la direction d'Armand Lanoux, études, notes et variantes, index établis par Henri Mitterand, Bibl. de la Pléiade, 5 vols, Paris, Gallimard, 1960-67 (Invaluable for detailed study).
3. *Contes et nouvelles,* texte établi, présenté et annoté par Roger Ripoll avec la collaboration de Sylvie Luneau pour les textes de Zola traduits du russe, Bibl. de la Pléiade, Paris, Gallimard, 1976.
4. *Le Roman expérimental,* chronologie et préface par Aimé Guedj, Paris, Garnier-Flammarion, 1971.
5. *Emile Zola: Carnets d'enquête: une ethnographie inédite de la France,* présentation d'Henri Mitterand, Coll. 'Terre Humaine', Paris, Plon, 1986 (Zola's documentation and preparatory notes).

BIBLIOGRAPHICAL INFORMATION

There is a vast critical literature of books and articles on Zola and on this novel. A very useful annotated bibliography will be found in

6. Brian Nelson, *Emile Zola: a selective analytical bibliography,* London, Grant & Cutler, 1982 (covers material published up to Jan. 1980).

For more comprehensive information see

7. David Baguley, *Bibliographie de la critique sur Emile Zola, 1864-1970* and the supplement for 1971-80, University of Toronto Press, 1976, 1982.

For recent books and articles, see *Cahiers naturalistes,* which, as well as being a mine of helpful critical material, publishes an annual bibliography. Critical surveys of twentieth-century Zola studies will be found in

8. Hemmings, F. W. J., 'The present position in Zola studies', *French Studies,* X, 2 (1956), 97-122 (covering the years 1920-56).
9. Lethbridge, Robert, 'Twenty years of Zola studies', *French Studies,* XXXI, 3 (1977), 281-93 (covering the years 1956-75).

See also Patrick Brady, 'A decade of Zola studies, 1976-85' in *24,* and the Introductions to *11* and *31.*

CRITICAL STUDIES

I list below only works referred to in this study, and some selected works published since 1985.

10. Auerbach, Erich, *Mimesis: the representation of reality in Western literature,* translated by W. R. Trask, Princeton University Press, 1953.
11. Baguley, D. (ed.). *Critical essays on Emile Zola,* Boston, Hall, 1986.
12. Baguley, D., *Naturalist Fiction: The Entropic Vision,* Cambridge University Press, 1990.
13. Becker, Colette (ed.), *Les Critiques de notre temps et... Zola,* Paris, Garnier, 1972.
14. Bernard, Marc, *Zola,* Coll. 'Ecrivains de toujours', Paris, Seuil, 1952 (Contains useful extracts from letters).
15. Borie, Jean, *Zola et les mythes,* Paris, Seuil, 1971.
16. Brooks, Peter, *The Melodramatic Imagination,* New Haven and London, Yale University Press, 1976.
17. Brown, Calvin S., *Repetitions in Zola's Novels,* Athens, Georgia, University of Georgia Press, 1952.
18. Butor, Michel, 'Emile Zola romancier expérimental de la flamme bleue' in *Repertoire, IV,* Paris, Minuit, 1974.
19. Buuren, Maarten van, *'Les Rougon-Macquart' d'Emile Zola: de la métaphore au mythe,* Paris, José Corti, 1986.
20. Descotes, Maurice, *Le Personnage de Napoléon III dans les 'Rougon-Macquart',* Coll. Archives des Lettres Modernes, Paris, Minard, 1970.
21. Dezalay, Auguste, *Lectures de Zola,* Paris, Armand Colin, 1973.
22. ———, *L'Opéra des 'Rougon-Macquart': essai de rythmologie romanesque,* Paris, Klincksieck, 1983.
23. Dubois, Jacques, *'L'Assommoir' de Zola, société, discours, idéologie,* Coll. 'Thèmes et textes', Paris, Larousse, 1973.
24. *L'Esprit Créateur,* special issue on Zola, XXV, 4, Winter 1985.
25. *Europe,* special issue on Zola (oct.-déc., 1952).
26. ———, special issue on Zola (avril-mai, 1968).
27. Hamon, Philippe, *Le Personnel du roman: le système des personnages dans les 'Rougon-Macquart' d'Emile Zola,* Geneva, Droz, 1983.

28. Hemmings, F. W. J., *Emile Zola* (2n ed.), Oxford University Press, 1966.
29. James, Henry, *The Critical Muse: selected literary criticism*, ed. Roger Gard, Harmondsworth, Penguin Books, 1987.
30. Lapp, J. C., *Zola before the 'Rougon-Macquart'*, University of Toronto Press, 1968.
31. Lethbridge, Robert and Keefe, Terry (ed.), *Zola and the Craft of Fiction: Essays in honour of F. W. J. Hemmings*, Leicester University Press, 1990.
32. Mitterand, Henri, *Zola et le naturalisme*, Coll. 'Que sais-je?', Paris, P.U.F., 1986.
33. ———, *Le Regard et le signe*, Paris, P.U.F., 1987.
34. Prendergast, Christopher, *Balzac, Fiction and Melodrama*, London, Edward Arnold, 1978.
35. Ripoll, Roger, *Réalité et mythe chez Zola*, 2 vols, Paris, Champion, 1981.
36. Schor, Naomi, *Zola's Crowds*, Johns Hopkins University Press, 1978.
37. Serres, Michel, *Feux et signaux de brume*, Paris, Grasset, 1975.
38. Toulouse, E., *Enquête médico-psychologique sur les rapports de la supériorité intellectuelle avec la névropathie: Emile Zola*, Paris, Société d'Editions Scientifiques, 1896.
39. Walker, Philip, *Zola*, London, Routledge & Kegan Paul, 1985.
40. Wilson, Angus, *Emile Zola*, London, Mercury Books, 1965.

CRITICAL GUIDES TO FRENCH TEXTS

edited by
Roger Little, Wolfgang van Emden, David Williams

61. **Geoffrey N. Bromiley**. Thomas's Tristan *and the* Folie Tristan d'Oxford.
62. **R.J. Howells**. Rousseau: Julie ou la Nouvelle Héloïse.
63. **George Evans**. Lesage: Crispin rival de son maître *and* Turcaret.
64. **Paul Reed**. Sartre: La Nausée.
65. **Roger McLure**. Sarraute: Le Planétarium.
66. **Denis Boak**. Sartre: Les Mots.
67. **Pamela M. Moores**. Vallès: L'Enfant.
68. **Simon Davies**. Laclos: Les Liaisons dangereuses.
69. **Keith Beaumont**. Jarry: Ubu Roi.
70. **G.J. Mallinson**. Molière: L'Avare.
71. **Susan Taylor-Horrex**. Verlaine: Fêtes galantes *and* Romances sans paroles.
72. **Malcolm Cook**. Lesage: Gil Blas.
73. **Sheila Bell**. Sarraute: Portrait d'un inconnu *and* Vous les entendez?
74. **W.D. Howarth**. Corneille: Le Cid.
75. **Peter Jimack**. Diderot: Supplément au Voyage de Bougainville.
76. **Christopher Lloyd**. Maupassant: Bel-Ami.
77. **David H. Walker**. Gide: Les Nourritures terrestres *and* La Symphonie pastorale
78. **Noël Peacock**. Molière: Les Femmes savantes.
79. **Jean H. Duffy**. Butor: La Modification.
80. **J.P. Little**. Genet: Les Nègres.
81. **John Campbell**. Racine: Britannicus.
82. **Malcolm Quainton**. D'Aubigné: Les Tragiques.
83. **Henry Phillips**. Racine: Mithridate.
84. **S. Beynon John**. Saint-Exupéry: Vol de nuit *and* Terre des hommes.
85. **John Trethewey**. Corneille: L'Illusion comique *and* Le Menteur.
86. **John Dunkley**. Beaumarchais: Le Barbier de Séville.
87. **Valerie Minogue**. Zola: L'Assommoir.
88. **Kathleen Hall**. Rabelais: Pantagruel *and* Gargantua.